PENGUIN BOOKS

IDENTITY AND VIOLENCE

'Closely argued, extremely well written and clearly the work of a highly civilized, cultivated and decent man . . . a model of its kind' *Spectator*

'A superb book – a great vision, deep understanding, muscular prose and dazzling relevance' *Asian Age*

'Lucid and convincing' Francis Fukuyama

'One of the few world intellectuals on whom we may rely to make sense out of our existential confusion' Nadine Gordimer

'The world's poor and dispossessed could have no more articulate or insightful a champion' Kofi Annan

'An important book whose lessons all thinking British Asians should absorb . . . one of the leading moral philosophers of our time' *Eastern Eye*

'Explains and encourages the need for tolerance, honest and constant self-questioning in the strange and anxious period we've found ourselves living in' *New Statesman*

ABOUT THE AUTHOR

Amartya Sen's books include *On Economic Inequality, Development as Freedom* and *The Argumentative Indian*. He won the 1998 Nobel Prize in economics. He is Lamont University Professor at Harvard and formerly Master of Trinity College, Cambridge. He lives in Cambridge, Massachusetts and Cambridge, England. His books have been translated into more than thirty languages.

IDENTITY AND VIOLENCE

THE ILLUSION OF DESTINY

Amartya Sen

PENGUIN BOOKS

PENGUIN BOOKS

Published by the Penguin Group
Penguin Books Ltd, 80 Strand, London WC2R 0RL, England
Penguin Group (USA) Inc., 375 Hudson Street, New York, New York 10014, USA
Penguin Group (Canada), 90 Eglinton Avenue East, Suite 700, Toronto, Ontario, Canada M4P 2Y3
(a division of Pearson Penguin Canada Inc.)
Penguin Ireland, 25 St Stephen's Green, Dublin 2, Ireland (a division of Penguin Books Ltd)
Penguin Group (Australia), 250 Camberwell Road,
Camberwell, Victoria 3124, Australia (a division of Pearson Australia Group Pty Ltd)
Penguin Books India Pvt Ltd, 11 Community Centre,
Panchsheel Park, New Delhi – 110 017, India
Penguin Group (NZ), 67 Apollo Drive, Rosedale, North Shore 0632, New Zealand
(a division of Pearson New Zealand Ltd)
Penguin Books (South Africa) (Pty) Ltd, 24 Sturdee Avenue,
Rosebank, Johannesburg 2196, South Africa

Penguin Books Ltd, Registered Offices: 80 Strand, London WC2R 0RL, England

www.penguin.com

First published in the United States of America by W. W. Norton & Co., Ltd 2006
First published in Great Britain by Allen Lane 2006
Published in Penguin Books 2007
1

Excerpts from "A Far Cry from Africa" and "Names" from *Collected Poems
1948–1984* by Derek Walcott copyright © Derek Walcott, 1986;
reprinted by permission of Faber and Faber Ltd. Excerpt from
"A Plea for Less Malice Toward None" by Ogden Nash copyright
1933 by Ogden Nash; reprinted by permission of Curtis Brown Ltd

Printed in Great Britain by Clays Ltd, St Ives plc

978–0–141–02780–7

To Antara, Nandana, Indrani, and Kabir
with the hope of a world less imprisoned by illusion

CONTENTS

PROLOGUE

Some years ago when I was returning to England from a short trip abroad (I was then Master of Trinity College in Cambridge), the immigration officer at Heathrow, who scrutinized my Indian passport rather thoroughly, posed a philosophical question of some intricacy. Looking at my home address on the immigration form (Master's Lodge, Trinity College, Cambridge), he asked me whether the Master, whose hospitality I evidently enjoyed, was a close friend of mine. This gave me pause since it was not altogether clear to me whether I could claim to be a friend of myself. On some reflection, I came to the conclusion that the answer must be yes, since I often treat myself in a fairly friendly way, and furthermore, when I say silly things, I can immediately see that with friends like me, I do not need any enemies. Since all this took some time to work out, the immigration officer wanted to know why exactly did I hesitate, and in particular whether there was some irregularity in my being in Britain.

Well, that practical issue was eventually resolved, but the conversation was a reminder, if one were needed, that identity can be a complicated matter. There is, of course, no great difficulty in persuading ourselves that an object is identical to itself. Wittgenstein, the great philosopher, once remarked that "there is no finer example of a useless proposition" than saying that something is identical to itself, but he went on to argue that the proposition, though completely useless, is nevertheless "connected with a certain play of the imagination."

When we shift our attention from the notion of *being identical to oneself* to that of *sharing an identity with others* of a particular group (which is the form the idea of social identity very often takes), the complexity increases further. Indeed, many contemporary political and social issues revolve around conflicting claims of disparate identities involving different groups, since the conception of identity influences, in many different ways, our thoughts and actions.

The violent events and atrocities of the last few years have ushered in a period of terrible confusion as well as dreadful conflicts. The politics of global confrontation is frequently seen as a corollary of religious or cultural divisions in the world. Indeed, the world is increasingly seen, if only implicitly, as a federation of religions or of civilizations, thereby ignoring all the other ways in which people see themselves. Underlying this line of thinking is the odd presumption that the people of the world can be uniquely categorized according to some *singular and overarching* system of partitioning. Civilizational or religious partitioning of the world population yields a "solitarist" approach to human identity, which sees human beings as members of exactly one group (in this case defined by civilization or religion, in contrast with earlier reliance on nationalities and classes).

A solitarist approach can be a good way of misunderstanding nearly everyone in the world. In our normal lives, we see ourselves as members of a variety of groups—we belong to all of them. The same person can be, without any contradiction, an American citizen, of Caribbean origin, with African ancestry, a Christian, a liberal, a woman, a vegetarian, a long-distance runner, a historian, a schoolteacher, a novelist, a feminist, a heterosexual, a believer in gay and lesbian rights, a theater lover, an environmental activist, a tennis fan, a jazz musician, and someone who is deeply committed to the view that there are intelligent beings in outer space with whom it is extremely urgent to talk (preferably in English). Each of these collectivities, to all of which this person simultaneously belongs, gives her a particular identity. None of them can be taken to be the person's only identity or singular membership category. Given our inescapably plural identities, we have to decide on the relative importance of our different associations and affiliations in any particular context.

Central to leading a human life, therefore, are the responsibilities of choice and reasoning. In contrast, violence is promoted by the cultivation of a sense of inevitability about some allegedly unique—often belligerent—identity that we are supposed to have and which apparently makes extensive demands on us (sometimes of a most disagreeable kind). The imposition of an allegedly unique identity is often a crucial component of the "martial art" of fomenting sectarian confrontation.

Unfortunately, many well-intentioned attempts to stop such violence are also handicapped by the perceived absence of choice about our identities, and this can seriously damage our ability to defeat violence. When the prospects of good relations among different human beings are seen (as they increasingly are) primarily in terms of "amity among civilizations," or "dialogue between religious groups," or "friendly relations between different communities" (ignoring the great many different ways in which people relate to each other), a serious miniaturization of human beings precedes the devised programs for peace.

Our shared humanity gets savagely challenged when the manifold divisions in the world are unified into one allegedly dominant system of classification—in terms of religion, or community, or culture, or nation, or civilization (treating each as uniquely powerful in the context of that particular approach to war and peace). The uniquely partitioned world is much more divisive than the universe of plural and diverse categories that shape the world in which we live. It goes not only against the old-fashioned belief that "we human beings are all much the same" (which tends to be ridiculed these days—not entirely without reason—as much too softheaded), but also against the less discussed but much more plausible understanding that we are *diversely different*. The hope of harmony in the contemporary world lies to a great extent in a clearer understanding of the pluralities of human identity, and in the appreciation that they cut across each other and work against a sharp separation along one single hardened line of impenetrable division.

Indeed, conceptual disarray, and not just nasty intentions, significantly contribute to the turmoil and barbarity we see around us. The illusion of destiny, particularly about some singular identity or other (and their alleged implications), nurtures violence in the world through omissions as well as commissions. We have to see clearly that we have many distinct affiliations and can interact with each other in a great many different ways (no matter what the instigators and their flustered opponents tell us). There is room for us to decide on our priorities.

The neglect of the plurality of our affiliations and of the need for choice and reasoning obscures the world in which we live. It pushes us in the direction of the terrifying prospects portrayed by Matthew Arnold in "Dover Beach":

> And we are here as on a darkling plain
> Swept with confused alarms of struggle and flight,
> Where ignorant armies clash by night.

We can do better than that.

PREFACE

Oscar Wilde made the enigmatic claim, "Most people are other people." This may sound like of one of his more outrageous conundrums, but in this case Wilde defended his view with considerable cogency: "Their thoughts are someone else's opinions, their lives a mimicry, their passions a quotation." We are indeed influenced to an amazing extent by people with whom we identify. Actively promoted sectarian hatreds can spread like wildfire, as we have seen recently in Kosovo, Bosnia, Rwanda, Timor, Israel, Palestine, Sudan, and many other places in the world. With suitable instigation, a fostered sense of identity with one group of people can be made into a powerful weapon to brutalize another.

Indeed, many of the conflicts and barbarities in the world are sustained through the illusion of a unique and choiceless identity. The art of constructing hatred takes the form of invoking the magical power of some allegedly predominant identity that drowns other affiliations, and in a conveniently bellicose form can also overpower any human sympathy or natural kindness that we may normally have. The result can be homespun elemental violence, or globally artful violence and terrorism.

In fact, a major source of potential conflict in the contemporary world is the presumption that people can be uniquely categorized based on religion or culture. The implicit belief in the

overarching power of a singular classification can make the world
thoroughly inflammable. A uniquely divisive view goes not only
against the old-fashioned belief that all human beings are much
the same but also against the less discussed but much more plausible understanding that we are diversely different. The world is
frequently taken to be a collection of religions (or of "civilizations"
or "cultures"), ignoring the other identities that people have and
value, involving class, gender, profession, language, science,
morals, and politics. This unique divisiveness is much more confrontational than the universe of plural and diverse classifications
that shape the world in which we actually live. The reductionism
of high theory can make a major contribution, often inadvertently,
to the violence of low politics.

   Also, global attempts to overcome such violence are often handicapped by a similar conceptual disarray, with the acceptance—
explicitly or by implication—of a unique identity forestalling many
of the obvious avenues of resistance. As a consequence, religion-
based violence might end up being challenged not through the
strengthening of civil society (obvious as that course is), but
through the deployment of different religious leaders of apparently
"moderate" persuasion who are charged with vanquishing the
extremists in an intrareligious battle, possibly through suitably
redefining the demands of the religion involved. When interper-
sonal relations are seen in singular intergroup terms, as "amity" or
"dialogue" among civilizations or religious ethnicities, paying no
attention to other groups to which the same persons also belong
(involving economic, social, political, or other cultural connections), then much of importance in human life is altogether lost,
and individuals are put into little boxes.

   The appalling effects of the miniaturization of people is the
subject matter of this book. They call for a reexamination and
reassessment of some well-established subjects, such as eco-

nomic globalization, political multiculturalism, historical post-
colonialism, social ethnicity, religious fundamentalism, and global
terrorism. The prospects of peace in the contemporary world may
well lie in the recognition of the plurality of our affiliations and in
the use of reasoning as common inhabitants of a wide world,
rather than making us into inmates rigidly incarcerated in little
containers. What we need, above all, is a clear-headed understanding of the importance of the freedom that we can have in
determining our priorities. And, related to that understanding, we
need an appropriate recognition of the role and efficacy of reasoned public voice—within nations and across the world.

The book began with six lectures I gave on identity at Boston
University between November 2001 and April 2002, in response
to a kind invitation from Professor David Fromkin of the Pardee
Center. The center is dedicated to the study of the future, and the
chosen title of the series of lectures was "The Future of Identity."
However, with a little help from T. S. Eliot, I was able to convince
myself that "Time present and time past, / Are both perhaps present in time future." By the time the book was done, it was as much
concerned with the role of identity in historical and contemporary
situations as with prognostications of hereafter.

In fact, two years before those Boston talks, in November
1998, I had given a public lecture at Oxford University on the role
of reasoning in the choice of identity, under the title "Reason
before Identity." Although the organization of the thoroughly formal "Romanes Lecture," delivered regularly at Oxford University
(William Gladstone had given the first one in 1892; Tony Blair
delivered the one in 1999), resulted in my being marched out of
the hall (in a procession led by university authorities in fancy
dress) as soon as the last sentence of the lecture had been aired
(before any listener could ask any question), I did eventually get
some helpful comments later on because of a little pamphlet that

was made out of the lecture. I have used the Romanes Lecture in writing this book and have drawn on my old text and also on the insights from the comments I received.

Indeed, I have benefited greatly from comments and suggestions after several other public lectures I gave on an array of related subjects (with some connection with identity) including, among others, the 2000 Annual Lecture at the British Academy, a special lecture at the College de France (hosted by Pierre Bourdieu), the Ishizaka Lectures in Tokyo, a public lecture at St. Paul's Cathedral, the Phya Prichanusat Memorial Lecture at Vajiravudh College in Bangkok, the Dorab Tata Lectures in Bombay and Delhi, the Eric Williams Lecture at the Central Bank of Trinidad and Tobago, the Gilbert Murray Lecture of OXFAM, the Hitchcock Lectures at the University of California at Berkeley, the Penrose Lecture at the American Philosophical Society, and the 2005 B.P. Lecture at the British Museum. I have also had helpful discussions following the presentations I have tried out over the last seven years, in different parts of the world: at Amherst College, the Chinese University of Hong Kong, Columbia University in New York, Dhaka University, Hitotsubashi University in Tokyo, Koc University in Istanbul, Mt. Holyoke College, New York University, Pavia University, Pierre Mendès France University in Grenoble, Rhodes University in Grahamstown, South Africa, Ritsumeikan University in Kyoto, Rovira Virgili University in Tarragona, Santa Clara University, Scripps College at Claremont, St. Paul's University, Technical University of Lisbon, Tokyo University, Toronto University, University of California at Santa Cruz, and Villanova University, in addition, of course, to Harvard University. These discussions have greatly helped me to work toward a better understanding of the problems involved.

For very useful comments and suggestions I am indebted to Bina Agarwal, George Akerlof, Sabina Alkire, Sudhir Anand,

Anthony Appiah, Homi Bhabha, Akeel Bilgrami, Sugata Bose, Lincoln Chen, Martha Chen, Meghnad Desai, Antara Dev Sen, Henry Finder, David Fromkin, Sakiko Fukuda-Parr, Francis Fukuyama, Henry Louis Gates Jr., Rounaq Jahan, Asma Jahangir, Devaki Jain, Ayesha Jalal, Ananya Kabir, Pratik Kanjilal, Sunil Khilnani, Alan Kirman, Seiichi Kondo, Sebastiano Maffetone, Jugnu Mohsin, Martha Nussbaum, Kenzaburo Oe, Siddiq Osmani, Robert Putnam, Mozaffar Qizilbash, Richard Parker, Kumar Rana, Ingrid Robeyns, Emma Rothschild, Carol Rovane, Zainab Salbi, Michael Sandel, Indrani Sen, Najam Sethi, Rehman Sobhan, Alfred Stepan, Kotaro Suzumura, Miriam Teschl, Shashi Tharoor, and Leon Wieseltier. My understanding of Mahatma Gandhi's ideas on identity has been immensely helped by my discussions with his grandson, Gopal Gandhi, writer and now the governor of West Bengal.

Robert Weil and Roby Harrington, my editors at Norton, have been immensely helpful with many important suggestions, and I have also benefited from discussions with Lynn Nesbit. Amy Robbins has done a superb job of copyediting my less-than-neat manuscript, and Tom Mayer has been wonderful in coordinating everything.

Aside from the supportive academic atmosphere at Harvard University where I teach, I have also benefited from the facilities at Trinity College, Cambridge, particularly during the summer months. The Centre for History and Economics at King's College, Cambridge, has helped me by providing a remarkably efficient research base; and I am most grateful to Inga Huld Markan for taking care of many research-related problems. Ananya Kabir's work at the center on related themes has also been of great use to me. For excellent research assistance, I am grateful to David Mericle and Rosie Vaughan. For meeting the material costs of my research activities, I am very grateful for joint support from the

Ford Foundation, the Rockefeller Foundation, and the Mellon Foundation.

Finally, I must also acknowledge the benefit I have received from wide-ranging discussions, involving participants from many different countries, at the World Civilization Forum, arranged by the Japanese Government in Tokyo in July 2005, which I was privileged to chair. I have also benefited from the 2004 discussions of Globus et Locus in Turin, led by Piero Bassetti, and the 2005 Symi Symposium held in July in Heraklion, Crete, on the related theme of global democracy, led by George Papandreou.

Even though the current public interest and engagement in issues of global violence are the results of terribly tragic and disturbing events, it is good that these matters are receiving widespread attention. Since I try to argue as strongly as I can for a wider use of our voice in the working of the global civil society (to be distinguished from military initiatives and strategic activities of governments and their alliances), I am encouraged by these interactive developments. I suppose that makes me an optimist, but much will depend on how we rise to the challenge that we face.

Amartya Sen
Cambridge, Massachusetts
October 2005

IDENTITY AND VIOLENCE

CHAPTER 1

THE VIOLENCE
OF ILLUSION

Langston Hughes, the African-American writer, describes in his 1940 autobiography, *The Big Sea*, the exhilaration that seized him as he left New York for Africa. He threw his American books into the sea: "[I]t was like throwing a million bricks out of my heart." He was on his way to his "Africa, Motherland of the negro people!" Soon he would experience "the real thing, to be touched and seen, not merely read about in a book."[1] A sense of identity can be a source not merely of pride and joy, but also of strength and confidence. It is not surprising that the idea of identity receives such widespread admiration, from popular advocacy of loving your neighbor to high theories of social capital and of communitarian self-definition.

And yet identity can also kill—and kill with abandon. A strong—and exclusive—sense of belonging to one group can in many cases carry with it the perception of distance and divergence from other groups. Within-group solidarity can help to feed between-group discord. We may suddenly be informed that we are not just Rwandans but specifically Hutus ("we hate Tutsis"), or that we are not really mere Yugoslavs but actually Serbs ("we absolutely don't like Muslims"). From my own childhood memory of Hindu-Muslim riots in the 1940s, linked with the politics of partition, I recollect the speed with which the broad human beings of January were suddenly transformed into the ruthless Hindus and fierce Muslims of July. Hundreds of thousands perished at the hands of people who, led by the commanders of carnage, killed others on behalf of their "own people." Violence is fomented by the imposition of singular and belligerent identities on gullible people, championed by proficient artisans of terror.

The sense of identity can make an important contribution to the strength and the warmth of our relations with others, such as neighbors, or members of the same community, or fellow citizens, or followers of the same religion. Our focus on particular identities can enrich our bonds and make us do many things for each other and can help to take us beyond our self-centered lives. The recent literature on "social capital," powerfully explored by Robert Putnam and others, has brought out clearly enough how an identity with others in the same social community can make the lives of all go much better in that community; a sense of belonging to a community is thus seen as a resource—like capital.[2] That understanding is important, but it has to be supplemented by a further recognition that a sense of identity can firmly exclude many people even as it warmly embraces others. The well-integrated community in which residents instinctively do absolutely wonderful things for each other with great immediacy and solidarity can be the very same community in which bricks are thrown through the windows of immigrants who move into the region from elsewhere.

The adversity of exclusion can be made to go hand in hand with the gifts of inclusion.

The cultivated violence associated with identity conflicts seems to repeat itself around the world with increasing persistence.[3] Even though the balance of power in Rwanda and Congo may have changed, the targeting of one group by another continues with much force. The marshaling of an aggressive Sudanese Islamic identity along with exploitation of racial divisions has led to the raping and killing of overpowered victims in the south of that appallingly militarized polity. Israel and Palestine continue to experience the fury of dichotomized identities ready to inflict hateful penalties on the other side. Al Qaeda relies heavily on cultivating and exploiting a militant Islamic identity specifically aimed against Western people.

And reports keep coming in, from Abu Ghraib and elsewhere, that the activities of some American or British soldiers sent out to fight for the cause of freedom and democracy included what is called a "softening-up" of prisoners in utterly inhuman ways. Unrestrained power over the lives of suspected enemy combatants, or presumed miscreants, sharply bifurcates the prisoners and the custodians across a hardened line of divisive identities ("they are a separate breed from us"). It seems to crowd out, often enough, any consideration of other, less confrontational features of the people on the opposite side of the breach, including, among other things, their shared membership of the human race.

Recognition of Competing Affiliations

If identity-based thinking can be amenable to such brutal manipulation, where can the remedy be found? It can hardly be sought in trying to suppress or stifle the invoking of identity in general. For one thing, identity can be a source of richness and warmth as well as of violence and terror, and it would make little sense to treat identity as a general evil. Rather, we have to draw on the understanding that the force of a bellicose identity can be challenged by the power of *competing* identities. These can, of course, include the broad commonality of our shared humanity, but also many other identities that everyone simultaneously has. This leads to other ways of classifying people, which can restrain the exploitation of a specifically aggressive use of one particular categorization.

A Hutu laborer from Kigali may be pressured to see himself only as a Hutu and incited to kill Tutsis, and yet he is not only a Hutu, but also a Kigalian, a Rwandan, an African, a laborer, and a human being. Along with the recognition of the plurality of our identities and their diverse implications, there is a critically important need to see the role of *choice* in determining the cogency and relevance of particular identities which are inescapably diverse.

That may be plain enough, but it is important to see that this illusion receives well-intentioned but rather disastrous support from practitioners of a variety of respected—and indeed highly respectable—schools of intellectual thought. They include, among others, dedicated communitarians who take the community identity to be peerless and paramount in a predetermined way, as if by nature, without any need for human volition (just "recognition"—to use a much-loved concept), and also unswerving cultural theorists who partition the people of the world into little boxes of disparate civilizations.

In our normal lives, we see ourselves as members of a variety of groups—we belong to all of them. A person's citizenship, residence, geographic origin, gender, class, politics, profession, employment, food habits, sports interests, taste in music, social commitments, etc., make us members of a variety of groups. Each of these collectivities, to all of which this person simultaneously belongs, gives her a particular identity. None of them can be taken to be the person's only identity or singular membership category.

Constraints and Freedoms

Many communitarian thinkers tend to argue that a dominant communal identity is only a matter of self-realization, not of choice. It is, however, hard to believe that a person really has no choice in deciding what relative importance to attach to the various groups to which he or she belongs, and that she must just "discover" her identities, as if it were a purely natural phenomenon (like determining whether it is day or night). In fact, we are all constantly making choices, if only implicitly, about the priorities to be attached to our different affiliations and associations. The freedom to determine our loyalties and priorities between the different groups to all of which we may belong is a peculiarly important liberty which we have reason to recognize, value, and defend.

The existence of choice does not, of course, indicate that there are no constraints restricting choice. Indeed, choices are always made within the limits of what are seen as feasible. The feasibilities in the case of identities will depend on individual characteristics and circumstances that determine the alternative possibilities open to us. This, however, is *not* a remarkable fact. It is just the way every choice in any field is actually faced. Indeed, nothing can be more elementary and universal than the fact that choices of all kinds in every area are always made within particular limits. For example, when we decide what to buy at the market, we can hardly ignore the fact that there are limits on how much we can spend. The "budget constraint," as economists call it, is omnipresent. The fact that every buyer has to make choices does not indicate that there is no budget constraint, but only that choices have to be made *within* the budget constraint the person faces.

What is true in elementary economics is also true in complex political and social decisions. Even when one is inescapably seen—by oneself as well as by others—as French, or Jewish, or Brazilian, or African-American, or (particularly in the context of the present-day turmoil) as an Arab or as a Muslim, one still has to decide what exact importance to attach to that identity over the relevance of other categories to which one also belongs.

Convincing Others

However, even when we are clear about how we want to see ourselves, we may still have difficulty in being able to persuade *others* to see us in just that way. A nonwhite person in apartheid-dominated South Africa could not insist that she be treated just as a human being, irrespective of her racial characteristics. She would typically have been placed in the category that the state and the dominant members of the society reserved for her. Our freedom to assert our personal identities can sometimes be extraordinarily limited in the eyes of others, no matter how we see ourselves.

Indeed, sometimes we may not even be fully aware how others identify us, which may differ from self-perception. There is an interesting lesson in an old Italian story—from the 1920s when support for fascist politics was spreading rapidly across Italy—

concerning a political recruiter from the Fascist Party arguing with a rural socialist that he should join the Fascist Party instead. "How can I," said the potential recruit, "join your party? My father was a socialist. My grandfather was a socialist. I cannot really join the Fascist Party." "What kind of an argument is this?" said the Fascist recruiter, reasonably enough. "What would you have done," he asked the rural socialist, "if your father had been a murderer and your grandfather had also been a murderer? What would you have done then?" "Ah, then," said the potential recruit, "then, of course, I would have joined the Fascist Party."

This may be a case of fairly reasonable, even benign, attribution, but quite often ascription goes with denigration, which is used to incite violence against the vilified person. "The Jew is a man," Jean-Paul Sartre argued in *Portrait of the Anti-Semite,* "whom other men look upon as a Jew; . . . it is the anti-Semite who *makes* the Jew." Charged attributions can incorporate two distinct but interrelated distortions: misdescription of people belonging to a targeted category, and an insistence that the misdescribed characteristics are the only relevant features of the targeted person's identity. In opposing external imposition, a person can both try to resist the ascription of particular characteristics and point to other identities a person has, much as Shylock attempted to do in Shakespeare's brilliantly cluttered story: "Hath not a Jew eyes? hath not a Jew hands, organs, dimensions, senses, affections, passions? fed with the same food, hurt with the same weapons, subject to the same diseases, healed by the same means, warmed and cooled by the same winter and summer, as a Christian is?"[5]

The assertion of human commonality has been a part of resistance to degrading attributions in different cultures at different points in time. In the Indian epic *Mahabharata,* dating from around two thousand years ago, Bharadvaja, an argumentative interlocutor, responds to the defense of the caste system by

Bhrigu (a pillar of the establishment) by asking: "We all seem to be affected by desire, anger, fear, sorrow, worry, hunger, and labor; how do we have caste differences then?"

The foundations of degradation include not only descriptive misrepresentation, but also the illusion of a singular identity that others must attribute to the person to be demeaned. "There used to be a me," Peter Sellers, the English actor, said in a famous interview, "but I had it surgically removed." That removal is challenging enough, but no less radical is the surgical implantation of a "real me" by others who are determined to make us different from what we think we are. Organized attribution can prepare the ground for persecution and burial.

Furthermore, even if in particular circumstances people have difficulty in convincing others to acknowledge the relevance of identities other than what is marshaled for the purpose of denigration (along with descriptive distortions of the ascribed identity), that is not reason enough to ignore those other identities when circumstances are different. This applies, for example, to Jewish people in Israel today, rather than in Germany in the 1930s. It would be a long-run victory of Nazism if the barbarities of the 1930s eliminated forever a Jewish person's freedom and ability to invoke any identity other than his or her Jewishness.

Similarly, the role of reasoned choice needs emphasis in resisting the ascription of singular identities and the recruitment of foot soldiers in the bloody campaign to terrorize targeted victims. Campaigns to switch perceived self-identities have been responsible for many atrocities in the world, making old friends into new enemies and odious sectarians into suddenly powerful political leaders. The need to recognize the role of reasoning and choice in identity-based thinking is thus both exacting and extremely important.

Denial of Choice and Responsibility

If choices do exist and yet it is assumed that they are not there, the use of reasoning may well be replaced by uncritical acceptance of conformist behavior, no matter how rejectable it may be. Typically, such conformism tends to have conservative implications, and works in the direction of shielding old customs and practices from intelligent scrutiny. Indeed, traditional inequalities, such as unequal treatment of women in sexist societies (and even violence against them), or discrimination against members of other racial groups, survive by the unquestioning acceptance of received beliefs (including the subservient roles of the traditional underdog). Many past practices and assumed identities have crumbled in response to questioning and scrutiny. Traditions can shift even within a particular country and culture. It is perhaps worth recollecting that John Stuart Mill's *The Subjection of Women,* published in 1874, was taken by many of his British readers to be the ultimate proof of his eccentricity, and as a matter of fact, interest in the subject was so minimal that this is the only book of Mill's on which his publisher lost money.[6]

However, the unquestioning acceptance of a social identity may not always have traditionalist implications. It can also involve a radical reorientation in identity which could then be sold as a piece of alleged "discovery" without reasoned choice. This can play an awesome role in the fomenting of violence. My disturbing memories of Hindu-Muslim riots in India in the 1940s, to which I referred earlier, include seeing—with the bewildered eyes of a child—the massive identity shifts that followed divisive politics. A great many persons' identities as Indians, as subcontinentals, as Asians, or as members of the human race, seemed to give way—

quite suddenly—to sectarian identification with Hindu, Muslim, or Sikh communities. The carnage that followed had much to do with elementary herd behavior by which people were made to "discover" their newly detected belligerent identities, without subjecting the process to critical examination. The same people were suddenly different.

Civilizational Incarceration

A remarkable use of imagined singularity can be found in the basic classificatory idea that serves as the intellectual background to the much-discussed thesis of "the clash of civilizations," which has been championed recently, particularly following the publication of Samuel Huntington's influential book, *The Clash of Civilizations and the Remaking of the World Order*.[7] The difficulty with this approach begins with unique categorization, well before the issue of a clash—or not—is even raised. Indeed, the thesis of a civilizational *clash* is conceptually parasitic on the commanding power of a unique *categorization* along so-called civilizational lines, which as it happens closely follows religious divisions to which singular attention is paid. Huntington contrasts Western civilization with "Islamic civilization," "Hindu civilization," "Buddhist civilization," and so on. The alleged confrontations of religious differences are incorporated into a sharply carpentered vision of one dominant and hardened divisiveness.

In fact, of course, the people of the world can be classified according to many other systems of partitioning, each of which has some—often far-reaching—relevance in our lives: such as nationalities, locations, classes, occupations, social status, languages, politics, and many others. While religious categories have received much airing in recent years, they cannot be presumed to obliterate other distinctions, and even less can they be seen as the only relevant system of classifying people across the globe. In partitioning the population of the world into those belonging to "the Islamic world," "the Western world," "the Hindu world," "the Buddhist world," the divisive power of classificatory priority is implicitly used to place people firmly inside a unique set of rigid boxes. Other divisions (say, between the rich and the poor, between members of different classes and occupations, between people of different politics, between distinct nationalities and residential locations, between language groups, etc.) are all submerged by this allegedly primal way of seeing the differences between people.

The difficulty with the thesis of the clash of civilizations begins well before we come to the issue of an inevitable clash; it begins with the presumption of the unique relevance of a singular classification. Indeed, the question "do civilizations clash?" is founded on the presumption that humanity can be preeminently classified into distinct and discrete civilizations, and that the relations *between different human beings* can somehow be seen, without serious loss of understanding, in terms of relations *between different civilizations*. The basic flaw of the thesis much precedes the point where it is asked whether civilizations must *clash*.

This reductionist view is typically combined, I am afraid, with a rather foggy perception of world history which overlooks, first, the extent of *internal* diversities within these civilizational categories, and second, the reach and influence of *interactions*— intellectual as well as material—that go right across the regional borders of so-called civilizations (more on this in chapter 3). And its power to befuddle can trap not only those who would like to support the thesis of a clash (varying from Western chauvinists to Islamic fundamentalists), but also those who would like to *dispute* it and yet try to respond within the straitjacket of its prespecified terms of reference.

The limitations of such civilization-based thinking can prove to be just as treacherous for programs of "dialogue among civilizations" (something that seems to be much sought after these days) as they are for theories of a clash of civilizations. The noble and elevating search for amity among people seen as amity between civilizations speedily reduces many-sided human beings into one dimension each and muzzles the variety of involvements that have provided rich and diverse grounds for cross-border interactions over many centuries, including the arts, literature, science, mathematics, games, trade, politics, and other arenas of shared human interest. Well-meaning attempts at pursuing global peace can have very counterproductive consequences when these attempts are founded on a fundamentally illusory understanding of the world of human beings.

More than a Federation of Religions

Increasing reliance on religion-based classification of the people of the world also tends to make the Western response to global terrorism and conflict peculiarly ham-handed. Respect for "other people" is shown by praising their religious books, rather than by taking note of the many-sided involvements and achievements, in nonreligious as well as religious fields, of different people in a globally interactive world. In confronting what is called "Islamic terrorism," in the muddled vocabulary of contemporary global politics, the intellectual force of Western policy is aimed quite substantially at trying to define—or redefine—Islam.

However, to focus just on the grand religious classification is not only to miss other significant concerns and ideas that move people, it also has the effect of generally magnifying the voice of religious authority. The Muslim clerics, for example, are then treated as the ex officio spokesmen for the so-called Islamic world, even though a great many people who happen to be Muslim by religion have profound differences with what is proposed by one mullah or another. Despite our *diverse diversities,* the world is suddenly seen not as a collection of people, but as a federation of religions and civilizations. In Britain a confounded view of what a multiethnic society must do has led to encouraging the development of state-financed Muslim schools, Hindu schools, Sikh schools, etc., to supplement preexisting state-supported Christian schools, and young children are powerfully placed in the domain of singular affiliations well before they have the ability to reason about different systems of identification that may compete for their attention. Earlier on, state-run denominational schools in Northern Ireland had fed the political distancing of Catholics and Protestants along one line of divisive categorization assigned at infancy, and the same predetermination of "discovered" identities is now being allowed and, in effect, encouraged to sow even more alienation among a different part of the British population.

Religious or civilizational classification can, of course, be a source of belligerent distortion as well. It can, for example, take the form of crude beliefs well exemplified by U.S. Lieutenant General William Boykin's blaring—and by now well-known—remark describing his battle against Muslims with disarming coarseness: "I knew that my God was bigger than his," and that the Christian God "was a real God, and [the Muslim's] was an idol."[8] The idiocy of such dense bigotry is, of course, easy to diagnose, and for this reason there is, I believe, comparatively limited danger in the uncouth hurling of such unguided missiles. There is, in contrast, a much more serious problem in the use in Western public policy of intellectual "guided missiles" that present a superficially nobler vision to woo Muslim activists away from opposition through the apparently benign strategy of defining Islam appropriately. They try to wrench Islamic terrorists from violence by insisting that Islam is a religion of peace, and that a "true Muslim" must be a tolerant individual ("so come off it and be peaceful"). The rejection of a confrontational view of Islam is certainly appropriate and extremely important at this time, but we must also ask whether it is at all necessary or useful, or even possible, to try to define in largely political terms what a "true Muslim" must be like.[9]

Muslims and Intellectual Diversity

A person's religion need not be his or her all-encompassing and exclusive identity. In particular, Islam, as a religion, does not obliterate responsible choice for Muslims in many spheres of life. Indeed, it is possible for one Muslim to take a confrontational view and another to be thoroughly tolerant of heterodoxy without either of them ceasing to be a Muslim for that reason alone.

The response to Islamic fundamentalism and to the terrorism linked with it also becomes particularly confused when there is a general failure to distinguish between Islamic history and the history of Muslim people. Muslims, like all other people in the world, have many different pursuits, and not all of their priorities and values need be placed within their singular identity of being Islamic (I shall go more into this issue in chapter 4). It is, of course, not surprising at all that the champions of Islamic fundamentalism would like to suppress all other identities of Muslims in favor of being only Islamic. But it is extremely odd that those who want to overcome the tensions and conflicts linked with Islamic fundamentalism also seem unable to see Muslim people in any form other than their being just Islamic, which is combined with attempts to redefine Islam, rather than seeing the many-dimensional nature of diverse human beings who happen to be Muslim.

People see themselves—and have reason to see themselves—in many different ways. For example, a Bangladeshi Muslim is not only a Muslim but also a Bengali and a Bangladeshi, typically quite proud of the Bengali language, literature, and music, not to mention the other identities he or she may have connected with class, gender, occupation, politics, aesthetic taste, and so on. Bangladesh's separation from Pakistan was not based on religion at all, since a Muslim identity was shared by the bulk of the population in the two wings of undivided Pakistan. The separatist issues related to language, literature, and politics.

Similarly, there is no empirical reason at all why champions of the Muslim past, or for that matter of the Arab heritage, have to concentrate specifically on religious beliefs only, and not also on science and mathematics, to which Arab and Muslim societies have contributed so much, and which can also be part of a Muslim or an Arab identity. Despite the importance of this heritage, crude classifications have tended to put science and mathematics in the basket of "Western science," leaving other people to mine their pride in religious depths. If the disaffected Arab activist today can take pride only in the purity of Islam, rather than in the many-sided richness of Arab history, the unique prioritization of religion, shared by warriors on both sides, plays a major part in incarcerating people within the enclosure of a singular identity.

Even the frantic Western search for "the moderate Muslim" confounds moderation in political beliefs with moderateness of religious faith. A person can have strong religious faith—Islamic or any other—along with tolerant politics. Emperor Saladin, who fought valiantly for Islam in the Crusades in the twelfth century, could offer, without any contradiction, an honored place in his Egyptian royal court to Maimonides as that distinguished Jewish philosopher fled an intolerant Europe. When, at the turn of the sixteenth century, the heretic Giordano Bruno was burned at the stake in Campo dei Fiori in Rome, the Great Mughal emperor Akbar (who was born a Muslim and died a Muslim) had just finished, in Agra, his large project of legally codifying minority rights, including religious freedom for all.

The point that needs particular attention is that while Akbar was free to pursue his liberal politics without ceasing to be a Muslim, that liberality was in no way ordained—nor of course prohibited—by Islam. Another Mughal emperor, Aurangzeb, could deny minority rights and persecute non-Muslims without, for that reason, failing to be a Muslim, in exactly the same way that Akbar did not terminate being a Muslim because of his tolerantly pluralist politics.

The Flames of Confusion

The insistence, if only implicitly, on a choiceless singularity of human identity not only diminishes us all, it also makes the world much more flammable. The alternative to the divisiveness of one preeminent categorization is not any unreal claim that we are all much the same. That we are not. Rather, the main hope of harmony in our troubled world lies in the plurality of our identities, which cut across each other and work against sharp divisions around one single hardened line of vehement division that allegedly cannot be resisted. Our shared humanity gets savagely challenged when our differences are narrowed into one devised system of uniquely powerful categorization.

Perhaps the worst impairment comes from the neglect—and denial—of the role of reasoning and choice, which follows from the recognition of our plural identities. The illusion of unique identity is much more divisive than the universe of plural and diverse classifications that characterize the world in which we actually live. The descriptive weakness of choiceless singularity has the effect of momentously impoverishing the power and reach of our social and political reasoning. The illusion of destiny exacts a remarkably heavy price.

CHAPTER 2

MAKING SENSE
OF IDENTITY

I n an arresting passage in *A Turn in the South,* V. S. Naipaul expresses a worry about losing one's past and one's historical identity in the melting pot of the present.

> In 1961, when I was travelling in the Caribbean for my first travel book, I remember my shock, my feeling of taint and spiritual annihilation, when I saw some of the Indians of Martinique, and began to understand that they have been swamped by Martinique, that I had no means of sharing the world view of these people whose history at some stage had been like mine, but who now, racially and in other ways, had become something other.[1]

Concerns of this kind not only indicate an anxiety and a disquiet, but also point illuminatingly to the positive and constructive importance people tend to attach to a shared history and a sense of affiliation based on this history.

And yet history and background are not the only way of seeing ourselves and the groups to which we belong. There are a great variety of categories to which we simultaneously belong. I can be, at the same time, an Asian, an Indian citizen, a Bengali with Bangladeshi ancestry, an American or British resident, an economist, a dabbler in philosophy, an author, a Sanskritist, a strong believer in secularism and democracy, a man, a feminist, a heterosexual, a defender of gay and lesbian rights, with a nonreligious lifestyle, from a Hindu background, a non-Brahmin, and a nonbeliever in an afterlife (and also, in case the question is asked, a nonbeliever in a "before-life" as well). This is just a small sample of diverse categories to each of which I may simultaneously belong— there are of course a great many other membership categories too which, depending on circumstances, can move and engage me.

Belonging to each one of the membership groups can be quite important, depending on the particular context. When they compete for attention and priority over each other (they need not always, since there may be no conflict between the demands of different loyalties), the person has to decide on the relative importance to attach to the respective identities, which will, again, depend on the exact context. There are two distinct issues here. First, the recognition that identities are robustly plural, and that the importance of one identity need not obliterate the importance of others. Second, a person has to make choices—explicitly or by implication—about what relative importance to attach, in a particular context, to the divergent loyalties and priorities that may compete for precedence.

Identifying with others, in various different ways, can be extremely important for living in a society. It has not, however, always been easy to persuade social analysts to accommodate identity in a satisfactory way. In particular, two different types of reductionism seem to abound in the formal literature of social and economic analysis. One may be called "identity disregard," and it takes the form of ignoring, or neglecting altogether, the influence of any sense of identity with others, on what we value and how we behave. For example, a good deal of contemporary economic theory proceeds as if, in choosing their aims, objectives, and priorities, people do not have—or pay attention to—any sense of identity with anyone other than themselves. John Donne may have warned, "No man is an island entire of itself," but the postulated human beings of pure economic theory are often made to see themselves as pretty "entire."

In contrast with "identity disregard," there is a different kind of reductionism, which we may call "singular affiliation," which takes the form of assuming that any person preeminently belongs, for all practical purposes, to one collectivity only—no more and no less. Of course, we do know in fact that any real human being belongs to many different groups, through birth, associations, and alliances. Each of these group identities can—and sometimes does—give the person a sense of affiliation and loyalty. Despite that, the assumption of singular affiliation is amazingly popular, if only implicitly, among several groups of social theorists. It seems to appeal often enough to communitarian thinkers as well as to those theorists of cultural politics who like to divide up the world population into civilizational categories. The intricacies of plural groups and multiple loyalties are obliterated by seeing each person as firmly embedded in exactly one affiliation, replacing the richness of leading an abundant human life with the formulaic narrowness of insisting that any person is "situated" in just one organic pack.

To be sure, the assumption of singularity is not only the staple nourishment of many theories of identity, it is also, as I discussed in the first chapter, a frequently used weapon of sectarian activists who want the targeted people to ignore altogether all other linkages that could moderate their loyalty to the specially marked herd. The incitement to ignore all affiliation and loyalties other than those emanating from one restrictive identity can be deeply delusive and also contribute to social tension and violence.[2]

Given the powerful presence of these two types of reductionism in contemporary social and economic thinking, both deserve serious attention.

Identity Disregard and the Rational Fool

I begin with identity disregard. The assumption of narrowly self-interested individuals has evidently appeared to be "natural" to many modern economists, and the oddity of that presumption has been made more extreme by the further insistence, which too is rather common, that this is what "rationality"—no less—invariably demands. There is an argument—an allegedly knockout argument—that we encounter too frequently. It takes the form of asking: "if it is not in your interest, why would you have chosen to do what you did?" This wise-guy skepticism makes huge idiots out of Mohandas Gandhi, Martin Luther King Jr., Mother Teresa, and Nelson Mandela, and rather smaller idiots out of the rest of us, by thoroughly ignoring the variety of motivations that move human beings living in a society, with various affiliations and commitments. The single-minded self-loving human being, who provides the behavioral foundations of a great many economic theories, has been adorned often enough by elevating nomenclature, such as being called "the economic man," or "the rational agent."

There have, of course, been critiques of the presumption of single-mindedly self-seeking economic behavior (even Adam Smith, who is frequently taken to be the founding father of "the economic man," had expressed profound skepticism of such an assumption), but much of modern economic theory tended to proceed as if these doubts were of marginal concern and could be easily brushed off.[3] In recent years these general critiques have, however, been supplemented by criticisms coming from results of experimental games and other behavioral tests, which have brought out serious tensions between the assumption of pure self-seeking with singular affiliation and how people are actually observed to behave. These observations have empirically reinforced conceptual doubts about the coherence and sustainability of the presumed mental makeup of such single-focus people because of the philosophical and psychological limitation involved in not being able to make any effective difference between entirely distinguishable questions: "what shall I do?" "what serves my interest best?" "what choices will best promote my objectives?" "what should I rationally choose?" A person who acts with impeccable consistency and predictability but can *never* give different answers to these disparate questions can be taken to be something of a "rational fool."[4]

It is, in this context, particularly important to try to incorporate the perception and understanding of identity into the characterization of preference and behavior in economics.[5] This has happened in many different ways in the recent literature. The inclusion of considerations of identity with others in a shared group—and the working of what George Akerlof, the economist, calls "loyalty filters"—can powerfully influence individual conduct as well as their interactions, which can take richly divergent forms.[6]

It must, of course, be recognized that the rejection of purely self-interested behavior does not indicate that one's actions are necessarily influenced by a sense of identity with others. It is quite possible that a person's behavior may be swayed by other types of considerations, such as her adherence to some norms of acceptable conduct (such as financial honesty or a sense of fairness), or by her sense of duty—or fiduciary responsibility—toward others with whom one does not identify in any obvious sense. Nevertheless, a sense of identity with others can be a very important—and rather complex—influence on one's behavior which can easily go against narrowly self-interested conduct.

That broad question also relates to another, to wit, the role of evolutionary selection of behavioral norms which can play an instrumentally important part.[7] If a sense of identity leads to group success, and through that to individual betterment, then those identity-sensitive behavioral modes may end up being multiplied and promoted. Indeed, both in *reflective* choice and in *evolutionary* selection, ideas of identity can be important, and mixtures of the two—combining critical reflection and selective evolution—can also, obviously, lead to the prevalence of identity-influenced behavior. The time has certainly come to displace the presumption of "identity disregard" from the exalted position it has tended to occupy in a substantial part of economic theory woven around the concept of "the economic man," and also in political, legal, and social theory (used in imitative admiration—a sincere form of flattery—of so-called rational-choice economics).

Plural Affiliations and Social Contexts

I turn now to the second type of reductionism: the assumption of singular affiliation. We are all individually involved in identities of various kinds in disparate contexts, in our own respective lives, arising from our background, or associations, or social activities.

This was discussed in the first chapter, but it is perhaps worth reemphasizing the point here. The same person can, for example, be a British citizen, of Malaysian origin, with Chinese racial characteristics, a stockbroker, a nonvegetarian, an asthmatic, a linguist, a bodybuilder, a poet, an opponent of abortion, a bird-watcher, an astrologer, and one who believes that God created Darwin to test the gullible.

We do belong to many different groups, in one way or another, and each of these collectivities can give a person a potentially important identity. We may have to decide whether a particular group to which we belong is—or is not—important for us. Two different, though interrelated, exercises are involved here: (1) deciding on what our relevant identities are, and (2) weighing the relative importance of these different identities. Both tasks demand reasoning and choice.

The search for a unique way of classifying people for social analysis is not, of course, new. Even the political grouping of people into workers and nonworkers, much used in classical socialist literature, had this simple feature. That such a two-class partition could be very deceptive for social and economic analysis (even for those with a commitment to the underdogs of society) is now widely acknowledged, and it is perhaps worth recollecting, in this context, that Karl Marx himself subjected this unique identification to severe criticism in his *Critique of the Gotha Programme*, in 1875 (a quarter century after *The Communist Manifesto*). Marx's critique of the German Workers Party's proposed plan of action (the "Gotha Programme") included an argument, among others, against seeing workers "only" as workers, ignoring their diversities as human beings:

> [U]nequal individuals (and they would not be different individuals if they were not unequal) are measurable only by an equal

standard in so far as they are brought under an equal point of view, are taken from one *definite* side only, *e.g.,* in the present case are regarded *only as workers,* and nothing more is seen in them, everything else being ignored.[8]

The singular-affiliation view would be hard to justify by the crude presumption that any person belongs to one group and one group only. Each of us patently belongs to many. But nor can that view be easily vindicated by claiming that despite the plurality of groups to which any person belongs, there is, in every situation, some one group that is naturally the preeminent collectivity for her, and she can have no choice in deciding on the relative importance of her different membership categories.

I shall have to come back to the question of multiple memberships and the role of choice in the idea of identity, but before that it is worth noting that in the variation of the relative importance of identities, there may be significant external influences as well: not everything turns specifically on the nature of reasoning and choice. This clarification is needed since the role of choice has to be understood after taking note of the other influences that restrict or restrain the choices one can make.

For one thing, the importance of a particular identity will depend on the social context. For example, when going to a dinner, one's identity as a vegetarian may be rather more crucial than one's identity as a linguist, whereas the latter may be particularly important if one considers going to a lecture on linguistic studies. This variability does nothing to rehabilitate the assumption of singular affiliation, but it illustrates the need to see the role of choice in a context-specific way.

Also, not all identities need have durable importance. Indeed, sometimes an identity group may have a very fleeting and highly contingent existence. Mort Sahl, the American comedian, is supposed to have responded to the intense tedium of a four-hour-long film, directed by Otto Preminger, called *Exodus* (the name was inspired by the ancient Jewish migration out of Egypt, led by Moses), by demanding on behalf of his fellow sufferers: "Otto, let my people go!" That group of tormented filmgoers did have reason for fellow feeling, but one can see the massive contrast between such an ephemeral group of "my people" and the well-knit and seriously tyrannized community of people led by Moses—the original subject of that famous entreaty.

To consider the acceptance issue first, classifications can take many different forms, and not all of the categories that can be consistently generated would serve as a plausible basis for an important identity. Consider the set of people in the world who were born between nine and ten in the morning, local time. This is a distinct and quite well-defined group, but it is hard to imagine that many people would get excited about sustaining the solidarity of such a group and the identity it could potentially produce. Similarly, people who wear size 8 shoes are typically not linked with each other with a strong sense of identity on that shoe-size ground (rather important as that descriptive specificity is, when it comes to buying shoes and, more importantly, trying cheerfully to walk around in them).

Classification is certainly cheap, but identity is not. More interestingly, whether a particular classification can plausibly generate a sense of identity or not must depend on social circumstances. For example, if size 8 shoes become extremely difficult to find for some complicated bureaucratic reason (to grasp the intelligibility of such a supply shortage, one might have to place oneself somewhere in Minsk or Pinsk at the high noon of Soviet civilization), then the need for shoes of that size may indeed become a shared predicament and can give reason enough for solidarity and identity. Social clubs might even be set up (preferably with a liquor license) to exchange information about the availability of size 8 shoes.

Similarly, if it were to emerge that people born between 9 and 10 A.M. are, for reasons we do not yet understand, particularly vulnerable to some specific ailment (Harvard Medical School might be marshaled to look into this), then again there is a shared quandary which can provide a reason for a sense of identity. To consider a different variant of this example, if some authoritarian ruler wants to curb the freedom of people born in that particular hour because of the ruler's supernatural belief in the perfidy of people born then (perhaps some Macbethian witches have told him that he will be killed by someone born between 9 and 10 A.M.), then again a case for solidarity and identity based on that classificatory unity and persecution may indeed emerge here.

Sometimes a classification that is hard to justify intellectually may nevertheless be made important through social arrangements. Pierre Bourdieu, the French philosopher and sociologist, has pointed out how a social action can end up "producing a difference when none existed," and "social magic can transform people by telling them that they are different." That is what competitive examinations do (the 300th candidate is still something, the 301st is nothing). In other words, the social world constitutes differences by the mere fact of designing them.[9]

Even when a categorization is arbitrary or capricious, once they are articulated and recognized in terms of dividing lines, the groups thus classified acquire derivative relevance (in the case of the civil service examination, it may involve the difference between having a fine job and having none), and this can be a plausible enough basis for identities on both sides of the separating line.

The reasoning in the choice of relevant identities must, therefore, go well beyond the purely intellectual into contingent social significance. Not only is reason involved in the choice of identity, but the reasoning may have to take note of the social context and contingent relevance of being in one category or another.

Contrasting and Noncontrasting Identities

We can also distinguish between "contrasting" and "noncontrasting" identities. The different groups may belong to the same category, dealing with the same kind of membership (such as citizenship), or to different categories (such as citizenship, profession, class, or gender). In the former case, there is some contrast between different groups within the same category, and thus between the different identities with which they are associated. But when we deal with groups classified on different bases (such as profession and citizenship, respectively), there may be no real contrast between them as far as "belonging" is concerned. However, even though these noncontrasting identities are not involved in any territorial dispute as far as "belonging" is concerned, they can compete with each other for our attention and priorities. When one has to do one thing or another, the loyalties can conflict between giving priority to, say, race, or religion, or political commitments, or professional obligations, or citizenship.

In fact, we can have plural identities even within contrasting categories. One citizenship does, in an elementary sense, contrast with another in a person's identity. But as this example itself indicates, even contrasting identities need not demand that one and one only of the unique specifications can survive, overthrowing all the other alternatives. A person can be a dual citizen of, say, both France and the United States. Citizenship can, of course, be made exclusive, as is the case with, say, China or Japan (this was, in fact, the case even with the United States until quite recently). But even when exclusivity is insisted on, the conflict of dual loyalty need not disappear. For example, if a Japanese citizen resident in Britain is unwilling to take British citizenship because she does not want to lose her Japanese national identity, she may still have quite a substantial loyalty to her British attachments and to other features of her British identity which no Japanese court can outlaw. Similarly, an erstwhile Japanese citizen who has given up that citizenship to become a UK citizen may still retain considerable loyalties to her sense of Japanese identity.

The conflict between the priorities and demands of different identities can be significant both for contrasting and for noncontrasting categories. It is not so much that a person has to deny one identity to give priority to another, but rather that a person with plural identities has to decide, in case of a conflict, on the relative importance of the different identities for the particular decision in question. Reasoning and scrutiny can thus play a major role both in the specification of identities and in thinking through the relative strengths of their respective claims.

Choice and Constraints

In each social context, there would be a number of potentially viable and relevant identities which one could assess in terms of their acceptability and their relative importance. In many situations, the plurality may become central because of the widespread relevance of durable and frequently invoked characteristics, such as nationality, language, ethnicity, politics, or profession. The person may have to decide on the relative significance of the different affiliations, which could vary depending on the context. It is quite hard to imagine that a person can really be bereft of the possibility of considering alternative identifications, and that she must just "discover" her identities, as if it were a purely natural phenomenon. In fact, we are all constantly making choices, if only implicitly, about priorities to be attached to our different affiliations and associations. Often such choices are quite explicit and carefully argued, as when Mohandas Gandhi deliberately decided to give priority to his identification with Indians seeking independence from the British rule over his identity as a trained barrister pursuing English legal justice, or when E. M. Forster famously concluded, "[I]f I had to choose between betraying my county and betraying my friend, I hope I should have the guts to betray my country."[10]

It seems unlikely that the thesis of singular affiliation can have any kind of plausibility given the constant presence of different categories and groups to which any human being belongs. It is possible that the often repeated belief, common among advocates of singular affiliation, that identity is a matter of "discovery" is encouraged by the fact that the choices we can make are constrained by feasibility (I cannot readily choose the identity of a blue-eyed teenage girl from Lapland who is entirely comfortable with six-month-long nights), and these constraints would rule out all kinds of alternatives as being nonfeasible. And yet even after that, there will remain choices to make, for example, between priorities of nationality, religion, language, political beliefs, or professional commitments. And the decisions can be momentous: for example, the father, Eugenio Colorni, of my late wife Eva had to weigh the divergent demands of being an Italian, a philosopher, an academic, a democrat, and a socialist, in Mussolini's fascist Italy in the 1930s, and chose to abandon the academic pursuit of philosophy to join the Italian resistance (he was killed by the fascists in Rome two days before American soldiers arrived there).

The constraints may be especially strict in defining the extent to which we can persuade *others,* in particular, to take us to be different from (or more than) what they insist on taking us to be. A Jewish person in Nazi Germany, or an African-American when faced with a lynch mob in the American South, or a rebellious, landless agricultural laborer threatened by a gunman hired by upper-caste landowners in North Bihar may not be able to alter his or her identity in the eyes of the aggressors. The freedom in choosing our identity in the eyes of others can sometimes be extraordinarily limited. This point is not in dispute.

Many years ago, when I was an undergraduate at Cambridge, one of my teachers, Joan Robinson, a superb professor of economics, told me (during a particularly argumentative tutorial—we used to have many of those): "The Japanese are too polite; you Indians are too rude; the Chinese are just right." I accepted this generalization immediately: the alternative would have been, of course, to give further evidence of the Indian propensity toward rudeness. But I also realized that no matter what I said or did, the imaging would not quickly change in my teacher's mind (Joan Robinson, by the way, was very fond of Indians: she thought that they were absolutely fine in a rude kind of way).

More generally, whether we are considering our identities as we ourselves see them or as others see us, we choose within particular constraints. But this is not in the least a surprising fact—it is rather just the way choices are faced in any situation. Choices of all kinds are always made within particular constraints, and this is perhaps the most elementary aspect of any choice. As was discussed in the first chapter, any student of economics knows that consumers always choose within a budget constraint, but that does not indicate that they have no choice, but only that they have to choose within their budgets.

There is also a need for reasoning in determining the demands and implications of identity-based thinking. It is clear enough that the way we see ourselves may well influence our practical reason, but it is by no means immediate how—indeed in which direction—that influence may work. A person may decide, on reflection, not only that she is a member of a particular ethnic group (for example, a Kurd), but also that this is an extremely important identity for her. This decision can easily influence the person in the direction of taking greater responsibility for the well-being and freedoms of that ethnic group—it can become for her an extension of the obligation to be self-reliant (the self now being extended to cover others in the group with which this person identifies).

However, this does not yet tell us whether the person should or should not favor members of this group in the choices she has to make. If, for example, she were to favor her own ethnic group in making public decisions, this could rightly be seen as a case of shady nepotism rather than an example of shining excellence of morality and ethics. Indeed, just as self-denial may be a part of public morality, it can even be argued that a person may have to be particularly diffident in favoring members of a group with which she identifies. There is no presumption that the recognition or assertion of an identity must necessarily be a ground for solidarity in practical decisions; this has to be a matter for further reasoning and scrutiny. Indeed, the need for reasoning is thoroughly pervasive at every stage of identity-based thoughts and decisions.

Communitarian Identity and the Possibility of Choice

I turn now to some specific arguments and claims, beginning with the alleged priority of one's community-based identity which has been forcefully advocated in communitarian philosophy. That line of thought not only prioritizes the importance of belonging to one particular community group rather than another, but often tends to see community membership as a kind of extension of one's own self.[11] Communitarian thinking has been in the ascendancy over the last few decades in contemporary social, political, and moral theorizing, and the dominant and compelling role of social identity in governing behavior as well as knowledge has been widely investigated and championed.[12]

In some versions of communitarian thinking, it is presumed— explicitly or by implication—that one's identity with one's community must be the principal or dominant (perhaps even the only significant) identity a person has. This conclusion can be linked to two alternative—related but distinct—lines of reasoning. One line argues that a person does not have access to other community-independent conceptions of identity and to other ways of thinking about identity. Her social background, firmly based on "community and culture," determines the feasible patterns of reasoning and ethics that are available to her. The second line of argument does not anchor the conclusion to perceptual constraints, but to the claim that identity is a matter of discovery anyway, and the communitarian identity will invariably be recognized to be of paramount importance, if any comparisons were to be made.

To look, first, at the thesis of severe perceptual limitation, it often takes the form of an amazingly strong assertion. In some of the more fervent versions of the thesis, we are told that we cannot invoke any criterion of rational behavior other than those that obtain in the community to which the person involved belongs. Any reference to rationality yields the retort, "*which* rationality?" or "*whose* rationality?" It is also argued not only that the *explanation* of a person's moral judgments must be based on the values and norms of the community to which the person belongs, but also that these judgments can be ethically assessed *only within* those values and norms, which entails a denial of the claims of competing norms on the person's attention. Various versions of these far-reaching claims have been forcefully aired and powerfully advocated.

This approach has had the effect of rejecting the feasibility of assessing—perhaps even comprehending—normative judgments about behavior and institutions across cultures and societies, and it has sometimes been used to undermine the possibility of serious cross-cultural exchange and understanding. This distancing sometimes serves a political purpose, for example, in the defense of particular customs and traditions on such matters as women's unequal social position or the use of particular modes of conventional punishment, varying from amputation to the stoning of allegedly adulterous women. There is an insistence here on splitting up the large world into little islands that are not within intellectual reach of each other.

These perceptual claims are certainly worth scrutinizing. There can be little doubt that the community or culture to which a person belongs can have a major influence on the way he or she sees a situation or views a decision. In any explanatory exercise, note has to be taken of local knowledge, regional norms, and particular perceptions and values that are common in a specific community.[13] The empirical case for this recognition is certainly strong. But this does not, in any plausible way, undermine or eliminate the possibility and role of choice and reasoning about identity. This is so for at least two specific reasons.

First, even though certain basic cultural attitudes and beliefs may *influence* the nature of our reasoning, they cannot invariably *determine* it fully. There are various influences on our reasoning, and we need not lose our ability to consider other ways of reasoning just because we identify with, and have been influenced by membership in, a particular group. Influence is not the same thing as complete determination, and choices do remain despite the existence—and importance—of cultural influences.

Second, the so-called cultures need not involve any *uniquely* defined set of attitudes and beliefs that can shape our reasoning. Indeed, many of these "cultures" contain considerable internal variations, and different attitudes and beliefs may be entertained within the same broadly defined culture. For example, Indian traditions are often taken to be intimately associated with religion, and indeed in many ways they are, and yet Sanskrit and Pali have a larger atheistic and agnostic literature than any other classical language: Greek or Roman or Hebrew or Arabic. When a doctrinal anthology such as the fourteenth-century Sanskrit book *Sarvadarshanasamgraha* (literally translated as "collection of all philosophies") presents sixteen chapters respectively sympathetic to sixteen different positions on religious issues (beginning with atheism), the aim is to cater to informed and discerning choice, rather than to indicate incomprehension of each other's positions.[14]

Our ability to think clearly may, of course, vary with training and talent, but we can, as adult and competent human beings, question and begin to challenge what has been taught to us if we are given the opportunity to do so. While particular circumstances may not sometimes encourage a person to engage in such questioning, the ability to doubt and to question is not beyond our reach.

The point is often made, plausibly enough, that one cannot reason from nowhere. But this does not imply that no matter what the antecedent associations of a person are, those associations must remain unchallenged, unrejectable, and permanent. The alternative to the "discovery" view is not choice from positions "unencumbered" with any identity (as some communitarian polemicists seem to imply), but choices that continue to exist even in any *encumbered* position one happens to occupy. Choice does not require jumping out of nowhere into somewhere, but it can lead to a move from one place to another.

Priorities and Reason

I turn now from the argument based on perceptual limitation to the other possible ground for relying on choiceless identities, to wit, the alleged centrality of discovery in "knowing who you are." As Michael Sandel, the political theorist, has illuminatingly explained this claim (among other communitarian claims), "[C]ommunity describes not just what they *have* as fellow citizens but also what they *are,* not a relationship they choose (as in a voluntary association) but an attachment they discover, not merely an attribute but a constituent of their identity."[15]

However, an enriching identity need not, in fact, be obtained only through discovering where we find ourselves. It can also be acquired and earned. When Lord Byron considered leaving Greece and parting from the people with whom this quintessential Englishman had come to identify so closely, he had reason to lament:

> Maid of Athens, ere we part,
> Give, oh, give me back my heart!

Byron's acquired identity with the Greeks vastly enriched his own life while also adding some strength to the Greek struggle for independence. We are not as imprisoned in our installed locations and affiliations as the advocates of the discovery view of identity seem to presume.

Perhaps, however, the strongest reason for being skeptical of the discovery view is that we have different ways of identifying ourselves even in our given locations. The sense of belonging to a community, while strong enough in many cases, need not obliterate—or overwhelm—other associations and affiliations. These choices are constantly faced (even though we may not spend all our time articulating the choices we are actually making).

Consider, for example, the Caribbean poet Derek Walcott's poem "A Far Cry from Africa," which captures the divergent pulls of his historical African background and his loyalty to the English language and the literary culture that goes with it (a very strong affiliation for Walcott):

> Where shall I turn, divided to the vein?
> I who have cursed
> The drunken officer of British rule, how choose
> Between this Africa and the English tongue I love?
> Betray them both, or give back what they give?
> How can I face such slaughter and be cool?
> How can I turn from Africa and live?

Walcott cannot simply "discover" what is his true identity; he has to decide what he should do, and how—and to what extent—to make room for the different loyalties in his life. We have to address the issue of conflict, real or imagined, and ask about the implications of our loyalty to divergent priorities and differentiated affinities. If Walcott wonders what conflict there is between his inseparable attachment to Africa and his love of the English language and his use of that language (indeed his astonishingly beautiful use of that language), that points to broader questions of disparate pulls on one's life. The presence of conflicting pulls is as real in France, or America, or South Africa, or India, or anywhere else, as it clearly is in Walcott's Caribbean. The basic seri-

ousness of the disparate pulls—of history, culture, language, politics, profession, family, comradeship, and so on—have to be adequately recognized, and they cannot all be drowned in a
single-minded celebration only of community.

The point at issue is not whether *any* identity whatever can be
chosen (that would be an absurd claim), but whether we do
indeed have choices over alternative identities or combinations of
identities, and perhaps more importantly, substantial freedom
regarding what *priority* to give to the various identities we may
simultaneously have.[16] To consider an illustration that was discussed in the last chapter, a person's choice may be constrained
by the recognition that she is, say, Jewish, but she still has a decision to make regarding what importance to give to that particular
identity over others that she may also have (related for example,
to her political beliefs, sense of nationality, humanitarian commitments, or professional attachments).

In the Bengali novel *Gora* by Rabindranath Tagore published
a century ago, the problematic hero, also called Gora, differs from
most of his friends and family in urban Bengal by strongly championing old-fashioned Hindu customs and traditions and is a
staunch religious conservative. However, Tagore places Gora in a
big confusion toward the end of the novel when his supposed
mother tells him that he was adopted as an infant orphan by the
Indian family after his Irish parents had been killed by the rebellious sepoys in the ferocious anti-British mutiny of 1857 (the
name Gora means "fair," and presumably his unusual looks had
received attention but no clear diagnosis). At one stroke, Gora's
militant conservatism is undermined by Tagore since Gora finds
all the doors of traditionalist temples closed to him—as a "foreign-
born"—thanks to the narrowly conservative cause which he himself had been championing.

We do discover many things about ourselves even when they

may not be as foundational as the one Gora had to face. But to recognize this is not the same as making identity just a matter of discovery. Even when the person discovers something very important about himself or herself, there are still issues of choice to be faced. Gora had to ask whether he should continue his championing of Hindu conservatism (though now from an inescapable distance) or see himself as something else. Gora chooses ultimately, helped by his girlfriend, to see himself just as a human being who is at home in India, not delineated by religion or caste or class or complexion. Important choices have to be made even when crucial discoveries occur. Life is not mere destiny.

CHAPTER 3

CIVILIZATIONAL CONFINEMENT

The "clash of civilizations" was already a popular topic well before the horrifying events of September 11 sharply added to the conflicts and distrust in the world. But these terrible happenings have had the effect of vastly magnifying the ongoing interest in the so-called clash of civilizations. Indeed, many influential commentators have been tempted to see an immediate linkage between observations of global conflicts and theories of civilizational confrontations. There has been much interest in the theory of civilizational clash forcefully presented in Samuel Huntington's famous book.[1] In particular, the theory of a clash between "Western" and "Islamic" civilizations has frequently been invoked.

There are two distinct difficulties with the theory of civilizational clash. The first, which is perhaps more fundamental, relates to the viability and significance of classifying people according to the civilizations to which they allegedly "belong." This question arises well before problems with the view that people thus classified into cartons of civilizations must be somehow antagonistic—the civilizations to which they belong are hostile to each other. Underlying the thesis of a civilizational clash lies a much more general idea of the possibility of seeing people primarily as belonging to one civilization or another. The relations between different persons in the world can be seen, in this reductionist approach, as relations between the respective civilizations to which they allegedly belong.

As was discussed in chapter 1, to see any person preeminently as a member of a civilization (for example, in Huntington's categorization, as a member of "the Western world," "the Islamic world," "the Hindu world," or "the Buddhist world") is already to reduce people to this one dimension. Thus, the deficiency of the clash thesis begins well before we get to the point of asking whether the disparate civilizations (among which the population of the world is neatly partitioned out) must necessarily—or even typically—clash. No matter what answer we give to that question, even by pursuing the question in this restrictive form, we implicitly give credibility to the allegedly unique importance of that one categorization over all the other ways in which people of the world can be classified.

Indeed, even the *opponents* of the theory of a "civilizational clash" can, in effect, contribute to propping up its intellectual foundation if they begin by accepting the same singular classification of the world population. The heartwarming belief in an underlying goodwill among people belonging to discrete civilizations is, of course, very different from the cold pessimism of seeing only conflict and strife between them. But the two approaches share the same reductionist conviction that human beings around the world can be understood and preeminently characterized in terms of the distinct civilizations to which they belong. The same pallid view of the world divided into boxes of civilizations is shared by both groups—warm and cold—of theorists.

For example, in disputing the gross and nasty generalization that members of the Islamic civilization have a belligerent culture, it is common enough to argue that they actually share a culture of peace and goodwill. But this simply replaces one stereotype with another, and furthermore, it involves accepting an implicit presumption that people who happen to be Muslim by religion would basically be similar in other ways as well. Aside from all the difficulties in defining civilizational categories as disparate and disjunctive units (on which more presently), the arguments on both sides suffer, in this case, from a shared faith in the presumption that seeing people exclusively, or primarily, in terms of the religion-based civilizations to which they are taken to belong is a good way of understanding human beings. Civilizational partitioning is a pervasively intrusive phenomenon in social analysis, stifling other—richer—ways of seeing people. It lays the foundations for misunderstanding nearly everyone in the world, even before going on to the drumbeats of a civilizational clash.

Singular Visions and the Appearance of Depth

If clashing civilizations is a remarkably grand thesis about conflicts, there are lesser, but also influential, claims that relate contrasts of cultures and identities to the conflicts and the profusion of atrocities we see in different parts of the world today. Instead of one majestically momentous partition that splits the world population into contending civilizations, as in Huntington's imagined universe, the lesser variants of the approach see local populations as being split into clashing groups with divergent cultures and disparate histories that tend, in an almost "natural" way, to breed enmity toward each other. Conflicts involving, say, Hutus and Tutsis, Serbs and Albanians, Tamils and Sinhalese, are then reinterpreted in lofty historical terms, seeing in them something that is much grander than the shabbiness of contemporary politics.

Modern conflicts, which cannot be adequately analyzed without going into contemporary events and machinations, are then interpreted as ancient feuds which allegedly place today's players in preordained roles in an allegedly ancestral play. As a result, the "civilizational" approach to contemporary conflicts (in grander or lesser versions) serves as a major intellectual barrier to focusing more fully on prevailing politics and to investigating the processes and dynamics of contemporary incitements to violence.

It is not hard to understand why the imposing civilizational approach appeals so much. It invokes the richness of history and the apparent depth and gravity of cultural analysis, and it seeks profundity in a way that an immediate political analysis of the "here and now"—seen as ordinary and mundane—would seem to lack. If I am disputing the civilizational approach, it is not because I don't see its intellectual temptations.

I am, in fact, reminded of an event fifty years ago, shortly after I first arrived in England from India, as a student at Cambridge University. A kindly fellow student, who had already acquired a reputation for insightful political analysis, took me to see the recently released film *Rear Window*, where I encountered a canny but crippled photographer, played by James Stewart, observing some very suspicious events in the house opposite. Like James Stewart, I too, in my naive kind of way, became convinced that a gruesome murder may have been committed in the apartment that could be seen from the rear window.

However, my theorist companion explained to me (amid whispered protests from neighbors urging him to shut up) that there was, he was certain, no murder at all, and that the whole film, I would soon discover, was a serious indictment of McCarthyism in America, which encouraged everyone to watch the activities of other people with great suspicion. "This is a robust critique," he informed this novice from the third world, "of the growing American culture of snooping." Such a critique, I could readily see, could have yielded quite a profound film, but I kept wondering whether it was, in fact, the film we were watching. Later on, I remember, I had to make a strong cup of coffee for my disappointed guide to Western culture to reconcile him to the shallow and trivial world in which the murderer got his mundane comeuppance. What must be similarly asked is whether in the world in which we live we are actually watching a grand clash of civilizations or something much more ordinary which merely looks like a civilizational clash to determined seekers of depth and profundity.

The depth that civilizational analysis seeks is not, however, exclusive to the high road of intellectual analysis. In some ways, civilizational analysis mirrors and magnifies common beliefs that flourish in not particularly intellectual circles. The invoking of, say, "Western" values against what "those others" believe is rather commonplace in public discussions, and it makes regular headlines in tabloids as well as figuring in political rhetoric and anti-immigrant oratory. In the aftermath of September 11, the stereotyping of Muslims came often enough from people who are no great specialists, if I am any judge, on the subject. But theories of civilizational clash have often provided allegedly sophisticated foundations of crude and coarse popular beliefs. Cultivated theory can bolster uncomplicated bigotry.

Two Difficulties of Civilizational Explanations

What, then, are the difficulties of explaining contemporary world events by invoking civilizational categories? Perhaps its most basic weakness lies, as was suggested in chapter 1, in its use of a particularly ambitious version of the illusion of singularity. To this has to be added a second problem: the crudeness with which the world civilizations are characterized, taking them to be more homogeneous and far more insular than tends to emerge from empirical analyses of the past and the present.

The illusion of singularity draws on the presumption that a person not be seen as an individual with many affiliations, nor as someone who belongs to many different groups, but just as a member of one particular collectivity, which gives him or her a uniquely important identity. The implicit belief in the overarching power of a singular classification is not just crude as an approach to description and prediction, it is also grossly confrontational in form and implication. A uniquely divisive view of the world population goes not only against the old-fashioned belief that "people are much the same the world over," but also against the important and informed understanding that we are different in many diverse ways. Our differences do not lie on one dimension only.

The realization that each of us can and do have many different identities related to different significant groups to which we simultaneously belong appears to some as a rather complicated idea. But, as was discussed in the last chapter, it is an extremely ordinary and elementary recognition. In our normal lives, we see ourselves as members of a variety of groups: we belong to all of them. The fact that a person is a woman does not conflict with her being a vegetarian, which does not militate against her being a lawyer, which does not prevent her from being a lover of jazz, or a heterosexual, or a supporter of gay and lesbian rights. Any person is a member of many different groups (without this being in any way a contradiction), and each of these collectivities, to all of which this person belongs, gives him or her a potential identity which—depending on the context—can be quite important.

The incendiary implications of crude and singular classifications were discussed earlier, and will be pursued further in the subsequent chapters. The conceptual weakness of the attempt to achieve a singular understanding of the people of the world through civilizational partitioning not only works against our shared humanity, but also undermines the diverse identities we all have which do not place us against each other along one uniquely rigid line of segregation. Misdescription and misconception can make the world more fragile than it need be.

In addition to the unsustainable reliance on the presumption of a singular categorization, the civilizational approach has tended to suffer also from ignoring the diversities within each identified civilization and also from overlooking the extensive interrelations between distinct civilizations. The descriptive poverty of the approach goes beyond its flawed reliance on singularity.

On Seeing India as a Hindu Civilization

Let me illustrate the issue by considering the way my own country, India, is treated in this classificatory system.[2] In describing India as a "Hindu civilization," Huntington's exposition of the alleged "clash of civilizations" has to downplay the fact that India has many more Muslims than any other country in the world with the exception of Indonesia and very marginally Pakistan. India may not be placed within the arbitrary definition of "the Muslim world," but it is still the case that India (with its 145 million Muslims—more than the whole British population and the entire French population put together) has a great many more Muslims than nearly every country in Huntington's definition of "the Muslim world." Also, it is impossible to think of the civilization of contemporary India without taking note of the major roles of Muslims in the history of the country.

It would be, in fact, quite futile to try to have an understanding of the nature and range of Indian art, literature, music, films, or food without seeing the range of contributions coming from both Hindus and Muslims in a thoroughly intermingled way.[3] Also, the interactions in everyday living, or in cultural activities, are not separated along communal lines. While we can, for example, contrast the style of Ravi Shankar, the magnificent sitarist, with Ali Akbar Khan, the great sarod player, on the basis of their particular mastery over different forms of Indian classical music, they would never be seen specifically as a "Hindu musician" or a "Muslim musician" respectively (even though Shankar does happen to be a Hindu and Khan a Muslim). The same applies to other fields of cultural creativity, including Bollywood—that great field of Indian mass culture—where many of the leading actors and actresses, as well as directors, come from a Muslim background (along with others with non-Muslim ancestry), and they are much adored by a population of which more than 80 percent happen to be Hindu.

Further, Muslims are not the only non-Hindu group in the Indian population. The Sikhs have a major presence, as do the Jains. India is not only the country of origin of Buddhism; the dominant religion of India was Buddhism for over a millennium, and the Chinese often referred to India as "the Buddhist kingdom."

Agnostic and atheistic schools of thought—the Carvaka and the Lokayata—have flourished in India from at least the sixth century B.C. to the present day. There have been large Christian communities in India from the fourth century—two hundred years before there were substantial Christian communities in Britain. Jews came to India shortly after the fall of Jerusalem; Parsees from the eighth century.

It is obvious that Huntington's characterization of India as a "Hindu civilization" has many descriptive difficulties. It is also politically combustible. It tends to add some highly deceptive credibility to the extraordinary distortion of history and manipulation of the present realities that Hindu sectarian politicians have tried to champion in trying to promote a "Hindu civilization" view of India. Huntington is indeed frequently quoted by many leaders of the politically active "Hindutva" movement, and this is hardly surprising given the similarity between his seeing India as a "Hindu civilization" and the promotion of a "Hindu view" of India that is so dear to the political gurus of Hindutva.

As it happens, in the general elections held in India in the spring of 2004, the coalition led by the Hindu activist party suffered a severe defeat, with fairly comprehensive reversals across the board. In addition to being headed by a Muslim president, the secular Republic of India now has a Sikh prime minister and a Christian president of the ruling party (not bad for the largest democratic electorate in the world with more than 80 percent Hindu voters). However, the threat of a renewed promotion of the Hindu sectarian conception of India is ever present. Even though the political parties committed to a Hindu view of India have received considerably less than a quarter of the votes (a smallish fraction of the Hindu population), political attempts at seeing India as a "Hindu civilization" will not easily die away. A simplistic characterization of India along an artificially singular religious line remains politically explosive, in addition to being descriptively flawed.

On the Alleged Uniqueness of Western Values

The portrayal of India as a Hindu civilization may be a crude mistake, but coarseness of one kind or another is present in the characterizations of other civilizations as well. Consider what is called "the Western civilization." Indeed, the champions of "the clash of civilizations," in line with the belief in the unique profundity of this singular line of division, tend to see tolerance as a special and enduring feature of Western civilization, extending way back into history. Indeed, this is seen as one of the important aspects of the clash of values that underpins the supposed clash of civilizations. Huntington insists that the "West was West long before it was modern."[4] He cites (among other allegedly special features such as "social pluralism") "a sense of individualism and a tradition of individual rights and liberties unique among civilized societies."

This increasingly common way of looking at civilizational divisions is not really as rooted in traditional cultural analysis in the West as it is sometimes supposed. For example, the characterization of Western culture in a world of other—very different—cultures that was presented by Oswald Spengler in his widely influential book *The Decline of the West* did make explicit room for heterogeneities within each culture and for the cross-cultural similarities that can be clearly observed. In fact, Spengler argued, "there is nothing preposterous in the idea of Socrates, Epicurus, and especially Diogenes, sitting by the Ganges, whereas Diogenes in a Western megalopolis would be an unimportant fool."[5]

Huntington's thesis is, in fact, very hard to sustain empirically.

Tolerance and liberty are certainly among the important achievements of modern Europe (leaving out some aberrations like Nazi Germany, or the intolerant governance of the British or French or Portuguese empires in Asia and Africa). But to see a unique line of historical division there—going back over the millennia—is quite fanciful. The championing of political liberty and of religious tolerance, in their full contemporary forms, is not an old historical feature of any country or civilization in the world. Plato and Aquinas were no less authoritarian in their thinking than was Confucius. This is not to deny that there were champions of tolerance in classical European thought, but even if this is taken to give credit to the whole Western world (from the ancient Greeks and Romans to the Vikings and the Ostrogoths), there are similar examples in other cultures as well.

For example, the Indian emperor Ashoka's dedicated championing of religious and other kinds of tolerance in the third century B.C. (arguing that "the sects of other people all deserve reverence for one reason or another") is certainly among the earliest political defenses of tolerance anywhere. The recent Bollywood movie *Ashoka* (made, as it happens, by a Muslim director) may or may not be accurate in all its details (there is, for one thing, fulsome use of Bollywood's fascination with singing, romancing, and economically dressed dancing), but it rightly emphasizes the importance of Ashoka's ideas on secularism and tolerance 2,300 years ago and their continuing relevance in the India of today. When a later Indian emperor, Akbar, the Great Mughal, was making similar pronouncements on religious tolerance in Agra from the 1590s onward (such as, "[N]o one should be interfered with on account of religion, and anyone is to be allowed to go over to a religion that pleases him"), the Inquisitions were quite extensive in Europe, and heretics were still being burned at the stake.

Global Roots of Democracy

Similarly, democracy is often seen as a quintessentially Western idea which is alien to the non-Western world. That civilizational simplification has received some encouragement recently from the difficulty that is being experienced by the U.S.-led coalition in establishing a democratic system of government in Iraq. However, there is a real loss of clarity when the blame for the difficulties in postintervention Iraq is not put on the peculiar nature of the underinformed and underreflected military intervention that was precipitately chosen, but placed instead on some imagined view that democracy does not suit Iraqi, or Middle Eastern, or non-Western cultures. That, I would argue, is a completely wrong way to try to understand the problems we face today—in the Middle East or anywhere else.

Doubts are often expressed that the Western countries can "impose" democracy on Iraq, or on any other country. However, to pose the question in that form—centering on the idea of "imposition"—implies a proprietary belief that democracy belongs to the West, taking it to be a quintessentially "Western" idea which has originated and flourished only in the West. This is a thoroughly misleading way of understanding the history and the contemporary prospects of democracy.

There can, of course, be no doubt at all that the modern concepts of democracy and public reasoning have been deeply influenced by European and American analyses and experiences over the last few centuries, particularly by the intellectual force of the European Enlightenment (including the contributions of such theorists of democracy as the Marquis de Condorcet, James Madison, Alexis de Tocqueville, and John Stuart Mill). But to extrapolate backward from these comparatively recent experiences to construct a quintessential and long-run dichotomy between the West and non-West would be very odd history.

In contrast with the specious history of redefining the long-run past on the basis of short-run experiences, there is an alternative—historically more ambitious—line of reasoning that focuses specifically on ancient Greece. The belief in the allegedly "Western" nature of democracy is often linked to the early practice of voting and elections in Greece, especially in Athens. The pioneering departure in ancient Greece was indeed momentous, but the jump from ancient Greece to the thesis of the allegedly "Western"—or "European"—nature of democracy is confusing and confounded for at least three distinct reasons.

First, there is the classificatory arbitrariness of defining civilizations in largely racial terms. In this way of looking at civilizational categories, no great difficulty is seen in considering the descendants of, say, Goths and Visigoths as proper inheritors of the Greek tradition ("they are all Europeans," we are told). But there is great reluctance in taking note of the Greek intellectual links with other ancient civilizations to the east or south of Greece, despite the greater interest the ancient Greeks themselves showed in talking to ancient Iranians, or Indians, or Egyptians (rather than in chatting up the ancient Ostrogoths).

The second issue concerns the follow-up of the early Greek experience. While Athens certainly was the pioneer in getting balloting started, there were many regional governments which went that way in the centuries to follow. There is nothing to indicate that the Greek experience in electoral governance had much *immediate* impact in the countries to the west of Greece and Rome, in, say, what is now France or Germany or Britain. In contrast, some of the contemporary cities in Asia—in Iran, Bactria, and India—incorporated elements of democracy in municipal governance in the centuries following the flowering of Athenian democracy. For example, for several centuries the city of Susa (or Shushan) in southwest Iran had an elected council, a popular assembly, and magistrates who were proposed by the council and elected by the assembly.

Third, democracy is not just about ballots and votes, but also about public deliberation and reasoning, what—to use an old phrase—is often called "government by discussion." While public reasoning did flourish in ancient Greece, it did so also in several other ancient civilizations—sometimes spectacularly so. For example, some of the earliest open general meetings aimed specifically at settling disputes between different points of view took place in India in the so-called Buddhist councils, where adherents of different points of view got together to argue out their differences. Emperor Ashoka, referred to earlier, who hosted the third—and largest—Buddhist council in the third century B.C. in the then capital of India, viz. Pataliputra (what is now Patna), also tried to codify and propagate what were among the earliest formulations of rules for public discussion (some kind of an early version of the nineteenth-century "Robert's rules of order").

The tradition of public discussion can be found across the world. To choose another historical example, in early seventh-century Japan, the Buddhist prince Shotoku, who was regent to his mother, Empress Suiko, insisted in "the constitution of seventeen articles," promulgated in A.D. 604: "Decisions on important matters should not be made by one person alone. They should be discussed with many." This, as it happens, is six hundred years earlier than the Magna Carta signed in the thirteenth century. The Japanese constitution of seventeen articles went on to explain the reason why plural reasoning was so important: "Nor let us be resentful when others differ from us. For all men have hearts, and each heart has its own leanings. Their right is our wrong, and our right is their wrong."[6] Not surprisingly, some commentators have seen in this seventh-century constitution Japan's "first step of gradual development toward democracy."[7]

There is a long history of public discussion across the world. Even the all-conquering Alexander was treated to a good example of public criticism as he roamed around in northwest India around 325 B.C. When Alexander asked a group of Jain philosophers why they were neglecting to pay any attention to the great conqueror (Alexander was clearly disappointed by these Indian philosophers' lack of interest in him), he received the following forceful reply:

> King Alexander, every man can possess only so much of the earth's surface as this we are standing on. You are but human like the rest of us, save that you are always busy and up to no good, travelling so many miles from your home, a nuisance to yourself and to others! . . . You will soon be dead, and then you will own just as much of the earth as will suffice to bury you.[8]

Middle Eastern history and the history of Muslim people also include a great many accounts of public discussion and political participation through dialogues. In Muslim kingdoms centered around Cairo, Baghdad, and Istanbul, or in Iran, India, or for that matter Spain, there were many champions of public discussion (such as Caliph Abd al-Rahman III of Córdoba in the tenth century, or Emperor Akbar of India in the sixteenth). I shall come back to this issue in the next chapter when discussing the systematic misinterpretation of Muslim history that can be found in the pronouncements both of religious fundamentalists and of Western cultural simplifiers.

The Western world has no proprietary right over democratic

ideas. While modern institutional forms of democracy are relatively new everywhere, the history of democracy in the form of public participation and reasoning is spread across the world. As Alexis de Tocqueville noted in 1835 in his classic book on democracy, while the "great democratic revolution" which he observed taking place in America could be seen, from one point of view, as "a new thing," it could also be seen, from a broader perspective, as a part of "the most continuous, ancient, and permanent tendency known to history."[9] Although Tocqueville confined his historical examples to Europe's past (pointing, for instance, to the powerful contribution toward democratization made by the admission of common people to the ranks of the clergy in "the state of France seven hundred years ago"), his general argument has immensely broader relevance.

In his autobiography *Long Walk to Freedom*, Nelson Mandela describes how influenced he was, as a young boy, by seeing the democratic nature of the proceedings of the local meetings held in his African hometown:

> Everyone who wanted to speak did so. It was democracy in its purest form. There may have been a hierarchy of importance among the speakers, but everyone was heard, chief and subject, warrior and medicine man, shopkeeper and farmer, landowner and laborer.[10]

Mandela's quest for democracy did not emerge from any Western "imposition." It began distinctly at his African home, though he did fight to "impose" it on "the Europeans" (as the white rulers in apartheid-based South Africa, it may be recollected, used to call themselves). Mandela's ultimate victory was a triumph of humanity—not of a specifically European idea.

Western Science and Global History

It is similarly important to see how so-called Western science draws on a world heritage. There is a chain of intellectual relations that link Western mathematics and science to a collection of distinctly non-Western practitioners. For example, the decimal system, which evolved in India in the early centuries of the first millennium, went to Europe at the end of that millennium via the Arabs. A large group of contributors from different non-Western societies—Chinese, Arab, Iranian, Indian, and others—influenced the science, mathematics, and philosophy that played a major part in the European Renaissance and, later, the Enlightenment.

Not only is the flowering of global science and technology not an exclusively Western-led phenomenon, there were major global advances in the world that involved extensive international encounters far away from Europe. Consider printing, which Francis Bacon put among the developments that "have changed the whole face and state of things throughout the world." Every one of the early attempts at developing the art of printing in the first millennium occurred far away from Europe. They were also, to a considerable extent, linked with the deep commitment of Buddhist intellectuals to public reading and the propagation of ideas, and indeed all the attempts at early printing in China, Korea, and Japan were undertaken by Buddhist technologists. Indian Buddhists, who tried to develop printing, in the seventh century, were less successful in this, but they did contribute the material that constituted the first dated printed book in the world, a Buddhist Sanskrit classic (*Vajracchedikaprajnaparamita*) popularly known as the *Diamond Sutra,* which was translated by a half-Indian, half-Turkish scholar from Sanskrit into Chinese in A.D. 402.

When the book was printed in Chinese in A.D. 868, it carried a motivational preface to the effect that it was being printed "for universal free distribution."[11]

It is right that there should be adequate acknowledgment of the tremendous progress of ideas and knowledge in Europe and America over the last few centuries. The Occident must get full credit for the major achievements that occurred in the Western world during the Renaissance, the Enlightenment, and the Industrial Revolution, which have transformed the nature of human civilization. But the presumption that all this is the result of the flowering of an entirely sequestered "Western civilization," developing in splendid isolation, would be a serious illusion.

Praising an imagined insularity does little justice to the way learning and thinking tend to progress in the world, drawing on developments in different regions. Ideas and knowledge cultivated in the West have, in recent centuries, dramatically changed the contemporary world, but it would be hard to see it as an immaculate Western conception.

Botched Abstractions and Foggy History

Reliance on civilizational partitioning is thoroughly flawed for at least two distinct reasons. First, there is a basic methodological problem involved in the implicit presumption that a civilizational partitioning is uniquely relevant and must drown—or swamp—other ways of identifying people. It is bad enough, though scarcely surprising, that those who foment global confrontations or local sectarian violence try to impose a prechosen single and divisive identity on people who are to be recruited as the "foot soldiers" of political brutality, but it is really sad to see that this blinkered vision gets significantly reinforced by the implicit support the anti-Western fundamentalist warriors get from theories bred in the Western countries of singular categorization of people of the world.

The second difficulty with civilizational partitioning used in this approach is that it is based on extraordinary descriptive crudeness and historical innocence. Many of the significant diversities within each civilization are effectively ignored, and interactions between them are substantially overlooked.

These twin failures produce a remarkably impoverished understanding of different civilizations and their similarities, connections, and interdependence in science, technology, mathematics, literature, trade, commerce, and political, economic, and social ideas. The foggy perception of global history yields an astonishingly limited view of each culture, including an oddly parochial reading of Western civilization.

CHAPTER 4

RELIGIOUS
AFFILIATIONS
AND MUSLIM
HISTORY

Recent theses about clashing civilizations have tended to draw much on religious difference as a central characteristic of differing cultures. However, aside from the conceptual flaw in seeing human beings in terms of only one affiliation and the historical mistake of overlooking the critically important inter-relations between what are assumed to be largely detached and discrete civilizations (both problems were discussed in the last chapter), these civilizational theories also suffer from having to overlook the heterogeneity of religious affiliations that character-ize most countries and, even more, most civilizations. The last problem can be quite a big one, too, since people of the same religion are frequently spread over many different countries and several distinct continents. For example, as was mentioned earlier, India may be seen by Samuel Huntington as a "Hindu civilization," but with nearly 150 million Muslim citizens, India is also among the three largest Muslim countries in the world. Religious categorization cannot be easily fitted into classifications of countries and civilizations.

This last problem can be overcome by classifying people not into lumpy civilizational units with religious correlates (like "Islamic civilization," "Hindu civilization," and such as in Huntington's categorization), but directly in terms of the religious groupings of people. This would lead to a neater and less defective classification, and it has, not surprisingly, appealed to many. Viewing individuals in terms of their religious affiliations has certainly become quite common in cultural analysis in recent years. Does this make the religion-centered analysis of the people of the world a helpful way of understanding humanity?

I have to argue that it does not. This may be a more coherent classification of the people of the world than civilized categorization, but it makes the same mistake of attempting to see human beings in terms of only one affiliation, viz. religion. In many contexts, such a classification can be rather helpful (for example, in determining the choice of religious holidays, or ensuring the safety of places of worship), but to take that to be the overarching basis of social, political, and cultural analysis in general would amount to overlooking all the other associations and loyalties any individual may have, and which could be significant in the person's behavior, identity, and self-understanding. The crucial need to take note of the plural identities of people and their choice of priorities survives the replacement of civilizational classifications with a directly religious categorization.

Indeed, the increasingly common use of religious identities

as the leading—or sole—principle of classification of the people of the world has led to much grossness of social analysis. There has been, in particular, a major loss of understanding in the failure to distinguish between (1) the various affiliations and loyalties a person who happens to be a Muslim has, and (2) his or her Islamic identity in particular. The Islamic identity can be one of the identities the person regards as important (perhaps even crucial), but without thereby denying that there are other identities that may also be significant. What is often called "the Islamic world" does, of course, have a preponderance of Muslims, but different persons who are all Muslims can and do vary greatly in other respects, such as political and social values, economic and literary pursuits, professional and philosophical involvements, attitude to the West, and so on. The global lines of division can be very differently drawn for these "other affiliations." To focus just on the simple religious classification is to miss the numerous—and varying—concerns that people who happen to be Muslim by religion tend to have.

The distinction can be extremely important, not least in a world in which Islamic fundamentalism and militancy have been powerful and in which Western opposition to them is often combined with a significant, if vaguely formulated, suspicion of Muslim people in general. Aside from the conceptual crudity reflected in that general attitude, it also overlooks the more obvious fact that Muslims differ sharply in their political and social beliefs. They also differ in their literary and artistic tastes, in their interest in science and mathematics, and even in the form and extent of their religiosity. While the urgency of immediate politics has led to a somewhat better understanding in the West of religious subcategories within Islam (such as the distinction between a person's being a Shia or a Sunni), there is a growing reluctance to go beyond them to take adequate note of the many nonreligious identities Muslim people, like other people in the world, have. But the ideas and priorities of Muslims on political, cultural, and social matters can diverge greatly.

Religious Identity and Cultural Variations

There can also be vast differences in the social behavior of different persons belonging to the same religion, even in fields often thought to be closely linked with religion. This is easy to illustrate in the contemporary world, for example, in contrasting the typical practices of traditionalist rural women in, say, Saudi Arabia and those of Muslim women in urban Turkey (where head scarves are rare, with dress codes that are often similar to those of European women). It can also be illustrated by noting the vast differences in the habits of socially active women in Bangladesh and the less outgoing women in more conservative circles in the very same country, even though the persons involved may all be Muslim by religion.

These differences must not, however, be seen simply as aspects of a new phenomenon that modernity has brought to Muslim people. The influence of other concerns, other identities, can be seen throughout the history of Muslim people. Consider a debate between two Muslims in the fourteenth century. Ibn Battuta, who was born in Tangier in 1304 and spent thirty years in various travels in Africa and Asia, was shocked by some of the things he saw in a part of the world that now lies between Mali and Ghana. In Iwaltan, not far from Timbuktu, Ibn Battuta befriended the Muslim qadi, who held an important civic office there.

Ibn Battuta records his disgust with the social behavior in the qadi's family:

> One day I went into the presence of the qadi of Iwaltan, after asking his permission to enter, and found with him a young and a remarkably beautiful woman. When I saw her I hesitated and wished to withdraw, but she laughed at me and experienced no shyness. The qadi said to me: "Why are you turning back? She is my friend." I was amazed at their behaviour.[1]

But the qadi was not the only one who shocked Ibn Battuta, and he was particularly censorious of Abu Muhammad Yandakan al-Musufi, who was a good Muslim and had earlier on actually visited Morocco himself. When Ibn Battuta visited him at his house, he found a woman conversing with a man seated on a couch. Ibn Battuta reports:

> I said to him: "Who is this woman?" He said: "She is my wife." I said: "What connection has the man with her?" He replied: "He is her friend." I said to him: "Do you acquiesce in this when you have lived in our country and become acquainted with the precepts of the Shariah?" He replied: "The association of women with men is agreeable to us and a part of good conduct, to which no suspicion attaches. They are not like the women of your country." I was astonished at his laxity. I left him and did not return thereafter. He invited me several times, but I did not accept.[2]

Note that Abu Muhammad's difference from Ibn Battuta does not lie in religion—they were both Muslim—but in their decision about right lifestyles.

Muslim Tolerance and Diversity

I turn now to a more political issue. Varying attitudes to religious tolerance have often been socially important in the history of the world, and much variation can be found in this respect among different persons all of whom are Muslim by religion. For example, Emperor Aurangzeb, who ascended to the Mughal throne in India in the late seventeenth century, is generally regarded as being rather intolerant; he even imposed special taxes on his non-Muslim subjects. And yet a very different attitude can be seen in the life and behavior of his elder brother Dara Shikoh, the eldest son (and legitimate heir) of Emperor Shah Jahan, and of Mumtaz Mahal, in whose memory the Taj Mahal would be built. Aurangzeb killed Dara to grab the throne. Dara was not only a student of Sanskrit and serious scholar in the study of Hinduism, it is his Persian translation, from Sanskrit, of the Hindu *Upanishads* which was for a century or more one of the main foundations of European interest in Hindu religious philosophy.

Dara and Aurangzeb's great-grandfather, Akbar, was extremely supportive of religious tolerance (as was discussed earlier), and he made it a recognized duty of the state to make sure that "no man should be interfered with on account of religion, and anyone is to be allowed to go over to a religion that pleases him." In line with his pursuit of what he called "the path of reason" (*rahi aql*), Akbar insisted in the 1590s on the need for open dialogue and free choice, and also arranged recurrent discussions involving not only mainstream Muslim and Hindu thinkers, but also Christians, Jews, Parsees, Jains, and even atheists.[3] Aside from Dara, Aurangzeb's own son, also called Akbar, rebelled against his father, and joined hands in this enterprise with the Hindu kingdoms in Rajasthan and later the Hindu Marathas (though Akbar's rebellion was ultimately crushed by Aurangzeb). While fighting from Rajasthan, Akbar wrote to his father protesting at his intolerance and vilification of his Hindu friends.[4]

Faced with such diversity among Muslims, those who can see no distinction between being a Muslim and having an Islamic identity would be tempted to ask: "Which is the correct view according to Islam? Is Islam in favor of such tolerance, or is it not? Which is it really?" The prior issue to be faced here is not what the right answer to this question is, but whether the question itself is the right one to ask. Being a Muslim is not an overarching identity that determines everything in which a person believes. For example, Emperor Akbar's tolerance and heterodoxy had supporters as well as detractors among the influential Muslim groups in Agra and Delhi in sixteenth-century India. Indeed, he faced considerable opposition from Muslim clerics. Yet when Akbar died in 1605, the Islamic theologian Abdul Haq, who was sharply critical of many of Akbar's tolerant beliefs, had to conclude that despite his "innovations," Akbar had remained a good Muslim.[5]

The point to recognize is that in dealing with this discrepancy, it is not necessary to establish that either Akbar or Aurangzeb was not a proper Muslim. They could both have been fine Muslims without sharing the same political attitudes or social and cultural identities. It is possible for one Muslim to take an intolerant view and another to be very tolerant of heterodoxy without either of them ceasing to be a Muslim for that reason. This is not only because the idea of *ijtehad,* or religious interpretation, allows considerable latitude within Islam itself, but also because an individual Muslim has much freedom to determine what other values and priorities he or she would choose without compromising a basic Islamic faith.

Nonreligious Concerns and Diverse Priorities

Given the present disaffection between Arab and Jewish politics, it is also worth remembering that there is a long history of mutual respect between the two groups. It was mentioned in the first chapter that when the Jewish philosopher Maimonides was forced to emigrate from an intolerant Europe in the twelfth century, he found a tolerant refuge in the Arab world. His host, who gave him an honored and influential position in his court in Cairo, was none other than Emperor Saladin, whose Muslim credentials can hardly be doubted, given his valiant role in the Crusades in fighting for Islam (Richard the Lionheart was one of his distinguished opponents).

Maimonides' experience was not, in fact, exceptional. Indeed, even though the contemporary world is full of examples of conflicts between Muslims and Jews, Muslim rulers in the Arab world and in medieval Spain had a long history of trying to integrate Jews as secure members of the social community whose liberties—and sometimes leadership roles—were respected. For instance, as María Rosa Menocal has noted in her book *The Ornament of the World,* by the tenth century the achievement of Córdoba in Muslim-ruled Spain in being "as serious a contender as Baghdad, perhaps more so, for the title of most civilized place on earth" was due to the constructive influence of the joint work of Caliph Abd al-Rahman III and his Jewish vizier, Hasdai ibn Shaprut.[6] Indeed, there is considerable evidence, as Menocal argues, that the position of Jews after the Muslim conquest "was in every respect an improvement, as they went from persecuted to protected minority."[7]

Our religious or civilizational identity may well be very important, but it is one membership among many. The question we have to ask is not whether Islam (or Hinduism or Christianity) is a peace-loving religion or a combative one ("tell us which it is really?"), but how a religious Muslim (or Hindu or Christian) may combine his or her religious beliefs or practices with other features of personal identity and other commitments and values (such as attitudes to peace and war). To see one's religious—or "civiliza-tional"—affiliation as an all-engulfing identity would be a deeply problematic diagnosis.

There have been fierce warriors as well as great champions of peace among devoted members of each religion, and rather than asking which one is the "true believer" and which one a "mere impostor," we should accept that one's religious faith does not in itself resolve all the decisions we have to make in our lives, includ-ing those concerning our political and social priorities and the cor-responding issues of conduct and action. Both the proponents of peace and tolerance and the patrons of war and intolerance can belong to the same religion, and may be (in their own ways) true believers, without this being seen as a contradiction. The domain of one's religious identity does not vanquish all other aspects of one's understanding and affiliation.

If being a Muslim were the only identity of anyone who hap-pens to be Muslim, then of course that religious identification would have to carry the huge burden of resolving a great many other choices a person faces in other parts of his or her life. But being Islamic can hardly be the only identity a Muslim has. Indeed, the denial of plurality as well as the rejection of choice in matters of identity can produce an astonishingly narrow and mis-directed view. Even the current divisions around the events of September 11 have placed Muslims on all sides of the dividing lines, and instead of asking which is the right Islamic position, we have to recognize that a Muslim can choose among several dif-ferent positions on matters involving political, moral, and social judgments without ceasing to be, for that reason, a Muslim.

Mathematics, Science, and Intellectual History

There have been many discussions of the fact that a great many Muslims died in the World Trade Center on 9/11. As persons working there, they did not evidently regard that to be an evil expression of Western civilization. The World Trade Center did, of course, have symbolic significance, with its massive height and advanced technology (using the new tubular concept of structural engineering), and could be seen—in politically bellicose eyes—as an expression of Western audacity. It is interesting, in this context, to recall that the principal engineer behind the tubular concept was Fazlur Rahman Khan, the Chicago-based engineer from Bangladesh, who did the basic work underlying the innovation and later on also designed several other tall buildings, such as the 110-story Sears Tower and the 100-story John Hancock Center in Chicago, and also the Hajj Terminal in Jeddah in Saudi Arabia. As it happens, he also fought for Bangladesh's independence from Pakistan in 1971 and wrote a very readable Bengali book on that war. The fact that Muslims are on different sides of many cultural and political divides should not be at all surprising if it is recognized that being a Muslim is not an all-engulfing identity.

It is also important to recognize that many intellectual contributions of Muslims which made a major difference to global knowledge were not in any sense purely Islamic contributions. Even today, when a modern mathematician at MIT or Princeton or Stanford invokes an "algorithm" to solve a difficult computational problem, she helps to commemorate the contributions of the ninth-century Arab mathematician al-Khwarizmi, from whose name the term "algorithm" is derived (the term "algebra" comes from his book *Al-Jabr wa al-Muqabalah*). Many other major developments in the history of mathematics, science, and technology were carried out by the Muslim intelligentsia.

Many of these developments reached Europe only at the beginning of the second millennium, when translations from Arabic to Latin became quite common. However, some influences on Europe came earlier through the Muslim rulers of Spain. To consider one example of technological advance, Muslim engineers, both Arab and Berber, were responsible for the development and use of the technology of irrigation in the form of *acequias* in Spain, drawing on the innovations they had introduced earlier in the dry lands in the Middle East. This allowed, more than a thousand years ago, the cultivation of crops, fruits and vegetables, and the pasturing of animals on what had earlier been completely dry European land. Indeed, Muslim technologists were in charge of this admirable technical job over many centuries.[8]

Furthermore, Muslim mathematicians and scientists had a significant role in the globalization of technical knowledge through the movement of ideas across the Old World. For example, the decimal system and some early results in trigonometry went from India to Europe in the early years of the second millennium, transmitted through the works of Arab and Iranian mathematicians. Also, the Latin versions of the mathematical results of Indian mathematicians Aryabhata, Varahamihira, and Brahmagupta, from their Sanskrit treatises produced between the fifth and seventh centuries, appeared in Europe through two distinct steps, going first from Sanskrit to Arabic and then to Latin (I shall return to such multicultural transmissions in chapter 7). As leaders of innovative thought in that period in history, Muslim intellectuals were among the most committed globalizers of science and mathematics. The religion of the people involved, whether Muslim or Hindu or Christian, made little difference to the scholarly commitments of these Muslim leaders of mathematics or science.

Similarly, many of the Western classics, particularly from ancient Greece, survived only through their Arabic translations, to be retranslated, mostly into Latin, in the early centuries of the second millennium, preceding the European Renaissance. The Arabic translations were originally made not, obviously, for preservation, but for contemporary use in the Arabic-speaking world— a world of some considerable expanse at the turn of the first millennium. But the global as well as domestic consequences that ultimately resulted from this process are entirely in line with what could be expected from the reach and catholicity of the scholarship of those who were leaders of world thought over those decisive centuries.

Plural Identities and Contemporary Politics

There are several reasons for which it is critically important today to pay attention to the distinction between (1) seeing Muslim people exclusively—or predominantly—in terms of their Islamic religion and (2) understanding them more broadly in terms of their many affiliations, which would certainly include their Islamic identity, but which need not crowd out the commitments that follow from their scientific interests, professional obligations, literary involvements, or political affiliations.

The first reason, of course, is the value of knowledge—the importance of knowing what is happening. Clarity of understanding has significance on its own, and can also have far-reaching consequences for thoughts and actions. For example, even when a gang of activists claim that their terrorist pursuits are particu-

larly ordained by Islamic injunctions, thereby trying to extend radically the reach of religious commands, we can certainly question
whether that is indeed the case. It would be an obvious and gross
mistake to go along with their failure to see the distinction
between an Islamic identity and the identity of being a dedicated
terrorist in what they see as the cause of Islam. To see this distinction does not, of course, foreclose the intellectual possibility
of debating whether Islamic injunctions can be interpreted in this
way, but the debate cannot even begin if the very distinction
between an Islamic identity and a Muslim person's many identities were entirely missed.

As it happens, most Muslim scholars would entirely reject the
claim that Islamic injunctions can require or sanction or even tol-
erate terrorism, even though many of them would also argue, as
will be discussed presently, that a person would not cease to be a
Muslim even if he were to interpret his duties differently (in the
view of their critics, mistakenly) so long as he adhered to the core
Islamic beliefs and practices. The first issue, however, is not to
confuse the role of a particular religious identity and the various
priorities a person of that particular religion may choose to have
(for a variety of other reasons).

Second, the distinction is of significance in the battle against
the politicization of religion, exemplified not only by the rapid
growth of political Islam, but also by the vigor with which the
politicization of other religions have proceeded (exemplified by the
political reach of "born-again" Christianity, or of Jewish extremism, or of the Hindutva movement). The world of practice—
indeed sometimes very nasty and brutally sectarian practice—is
systematically fed by the confusion between having a religion and
ignoring the need for reasoning—and for freedom of thought—in
deciding on matters that need not be "locked up" by religious faith.
The process of misbegotten politicization can be seen, to varying

extents, in the increasingly polarized world, and it can vary from contributing directly to recruitment for active terrorism to enhancing vulnerability to such recruitment or encouraging tolerance of violence in the name of religion.

For example, the "creeping Shariah-ization of Indonesia," which the Indonesian Muslim scholar Syafi'i Anwar has described with much alarm, not only is a development of religious practice, but involves the spread of a particularly pugnacious social and political perspective in a traditionally tolerant—and richly multicultural—country.[9] A similar thing can be said about a number of other countries, including Malaysia, which have experienced a rapid promotion of a confrontational culture in the name of Islam, despite their history of cultural diversity and political breadth. To resist political polarization, this foundational distinction has to be pressed, since the exploitation of a religious (in this case, Islamic) identity is such a big part of the cultivation of organized conflicts of this kind.[10]

Third, the distinction allows us to understand more fully what is going on internally in countries that are placed by outsiders in some religious box, such as the so-called Islamic world, as if that identification could comprehensively explain current intellectual developments there. It is important to recognize that many countries that are formally Islamic states have ongoing political struggles in which many of the protagonists, even when they are devout Muslims by religion, do not draw their arguments only from their Islamic identity.

Consider Pakistan, which is certainly an Islamic state, and has Islam as its state religion with various political implications (for example, a non-Muslim could not be elected president of the country no matter how many votes he or she could get). And yet the civil society in that intellectually active country makes room for many commitments and pursuits that are not derived primarily—

or at all—from religion. For example, Pakistan has a dedicated, and in many ways highly successful, Human Rights Commission, which appeals not just to Islamic entitlements but also to more broadly defined human rights. Even though, unlike the Human Rights Commission of India or South Africa, which are recognized bodies with legal power, the commission in Pakistan has no legal or constitutional standing (indeed it is formally no more than an NGO), yet under the stewardship of visionary leaders of civil society such as Asma Jahangir and I. A. Rehman, it has done much to fight for the freedoms of women, minorities, and other threatened people. Its qualified success has been based on the use of Pakistan's civil laws (to the extent that they have not been maimed by extremist reform), the courage and commitment of civil dissidents, the fair-mindedness of many upright members of the judiciary, the presence of a large body of socially progressive public opinion, and, last but not least, the effectiveness of the media in drawing attention to inhumanity and violation of civil decency. In fact, Pakistan's media, like the Bangladeshi press, has also been very active in directly investigating and prominently reporting cases of abuse and in raising humane—and often secular—issues for the attention of a reflective public.[11]

These recognitions do not reduce in any way the need to deal with "the depths of Pakistan's problem with Islamic extremism," as Husain Haqqani, a former Pakistani ambassador to Sri Lanka, has put it. It is critically important to pay attention to the diagnosis Haqqani has presented persuasively that "the disproportionate influence wielded by fundamentalist groups in Pakistan is the result of state sponsorship of such groups," and to his warning that "an environment dominated by Islamist and militarist ideologies is the ideal breeding ground for radicals and exportable radicalism."[12] These issues have to be addressed at different levels, and call for the reforming of governance and the military, the pressing for democratic rights, giving more freedom of operation to the nonreligious and nonextremist political parties, and dealing with training grounds and fundamentalist schools that incline students toward confrontation and militancy. But attention must also be paid to the ongoing struggle within Pakistan in which its strong intellectual community has been playing a valuable, often visionary, role. Indeed, Husain Haqqani's own penetrating analysis is part of this richly constructive movement. The American-led "war on terror" has been so preoccupied with military moves, interstate diplomacy, intergovernment dialogues, and working with rulers in general (across the world, not just in Pakistan) that there has tended to be a serious neglect of the importance of civil society, despite the critically important work that it does in very difficult circumstances.

Indeed, humanist pursuits of broad reach have a rich history in Pakistan, and this tradition deserves celebration and support. It has already produced much-admired results that have received global attention in other contexts. For example, the human development approach to understanding economic and social progress (judging progress not merely by the growth of gross national product but by the enhancement of people's living conditions) has been pioneered in the world by a Pakistani economist and former finance minister, Mahbub ul Haq.[13] The approach has been widely used internationally, including in Pakistan, to assess the deficiencies of public policies (the critique has often been blistering), and it still remains one of the mainstays of the United Nations' constructive efforts in economic and social development. It is important to recognize that A. Q. Khan's clandestine nuclear wares are not the only things Pakistan has exported abroad.

Momentous nondenominational contributions of this kind draw on the broad visions of the persons involved, not specifically on their religiosity. And yet this fact did not make Mahbub ul Haq any less of a Muslim. His faith in religion in its proper domain was strong, as I can confirm, having had the privilege of knowing him as a close friend (from our days together as undergraduates at Cambridge in the early 1950s to his sudden death in 1998). The distinction between the broad variety of commitments of Muslims and their narrowly defined Islamic identity in particular is extraordinarily important to understand.

The fourth reason for emphasizing the importance of this distinction is that it is significantly—and sometimes entirely—missed in some of the "battles against terrorism" that are currently being waged. This can, and I believe already does, have very counterproductive effects. For example, attempts to fight terrorism through recruiting religion "on one's side" has not only been quite ineffective, they also suffer, I would argue, from a serious conceptual disorientation. This subject clearly deserves a fuller discussion.

Fighting Terrorism and Understanding Identities

The confusion between the plural identities of Muslims and their Islamic identity in particular is not only a descriptive mistake, it has serious implications for policies for peace in the precarious world in which we live. There is a great deal of anxiety in the contemporary world about global conflicts and terrorism. This is as it should be, since the threats are real and the need to do something to overcome and subdue these dangers is urgent. The actions taken in recent years have included military interventions in Afghanistan and Iraq. These are important subjects for public debate (I must confess that I have been totally skeptical of the policies chosen by the coalition partners for the Iraq operation in particular), but my focus here will be on another part of the global approach to conflicts and terrorism, involving public policies related to cultural relations and civil society.

As was discussed in the first chapter, this book is especially concerned with the conceptual framework within which these confrontations are seen and understood, and how the demands of public action are interpreted. A confusing role is played here by the reliance on a single categorization of the people of the world. The confusion adds to the flammability of the world in which we live. The problem I am referring to is much more subtle than the crude and abusive views that have been expressed about other cultures by people in the West, like the irrepressible Lieutenant General William Boykin of the U.S. Army (whose claim that the Christian God was "bigger than" the Islamic God was discussed in the first chapter). It is easy to see the obtuseness and inanity of views of this kind.

What, however, can be seen as a bigger and more general problem (despite the absence of the grossness of vilification) are the possibly terrible consequences of classifying people in terms of singular affiliations woven around exclusively religious identities. This is especially critical for understanding the nature and dynamics of global violence and terrorism in the contemporary world. The religious partitioning of the world produces a deeply misleading understanding of the people across the world and the diverse relations between them, and it also has the effect of magnifying one particular distinction between one person and another to the exclusion of all other important concerns.

In dealing with what is called "Islamic terrorism," there have been debates on whether being a Muslim demands some kind of strongly confrontational militancy, or whether, as many world leaders have argued in a warm—and even inspiring—way, a "true Muslim" must be a tolerant individual. The denial of the necessity of a confrontational reading of Islam is certainly appropriate and extremely important today, and Tony Blair in particular deserves much applause for what he has done in this respect. But in the context of Blair's frequent invoking of "the moderate and true voice of Islam," we have to ask whether it is at all possible—or necessary—to define a "true Muslim" in terms of political and social beliefs about confrontation and tolerance, on which different Muslims have historically taken, as was discussed earlier, very different positions. The effect of this religion-centered political approach, and of the institutional policies it has generated (with frequent announcements of the kind, to cite one example, "the government is meeting Muslim leaders in the next vital stage designed to cement a united front"), has been to bolster and strengthen the voice of religious authorities while downgrading the importance of nonreligious institutions and movements.

The difficulty with acting on the presumption of a singular identity—that of religion—is not, of course, a special problem applying only to Muslims. It would also apply to any attempt to understand the political views and social judgments of people who happen to be Christian, or Jewish, or Hindu, or Sikh, by relying mainly—or only—on what their alleged religious leaders declare as spokesmen for their "flocks." The singular classification gives a commanding voice to the "establishment" figures in the respective religious hierarchy while other perspectives are relatively downgraded and eclipsed.

There is concern—and some astonishment—today that despite attempts to bring in the religious establishment of Muslims and other non-Christian groups into dialogues about global peace and local calm, religious fundamentalism and militant recruitment have continued to flourish even in Western countries. And yet this should not have come as a surprise. Trying to recruit religious leaders and clerics in support of political causes, along with trying to redefine the religions involved in terms of political and social attitudes, downplays the significance of nonreligious values people can and do have in their appropriate domain, whether or not they are religious.

The efforts to recruit the mullahs and the clergy to play a role outside the immediate province of religion could, of course, make some difference in what is preached in mosques or temples. But it also downgrades the civic initiatives people who happen to be Muslim by religion can and do undertake (along with others) to deal with what are essentially political and social problems. Further, it also heightens the sense of distance between members of different religious communities by playing up their religious differences in particular, often at the cost of other identities (including that of being a citizen of the country in question), which could have had a more uniting role. Should a British citizen who happens to be Muslim have to rely on clerics or other leaders of the religious community to communicate with the prime minister of his country, who has been particularly keen to speak through the religious leaders?

It should not be so surprising that the overlooking of all the identities of people other than those connected with religion can prove to be a problematic way of trying to reduce the hold of religious sectarianism. This problem also arises sharply in dealing with the more difficult—and more turbulent—political situation in battle-torn Iraq and Afghanistan. The elections and referendum in Iraq in 2005 can be seen as a considerable success within their own criteria of assessment: the elections did occur, a fairly high proportion of the electorate did vote, and violent interruptions did not mar the entire effort. And yet in the absence of opportunities for open and participatory dialogue beyond what was provided by religious institutions, the voting process was predictably sectarian, linked with religious and ethnic denominations. The participation of people from different denominations (Shia, Sunni, Kurd) seemed to be rigidly intermediated by the spokesmen for the respective denominations, with the general citizenship roles of those people being given little opportunity to develop and flourish.

Despite many achievements of the Karzai government in Kabul (certainly much has been accomplished), there is a somewhat similar, if less intense, problem in Afghanistan as well, with the attempted reliance in official policy on gatherings of tribal leaders and councils of clerics, rather than on the more exacting, but critically important, cultivation of open general dialogues and interactions that could go beyond religious politics. To see religious affiliation as an all-engulfing identity can take a considerable political toll. Given the tremendous challenges the Afghan leadership faces, it is necessary to be patient with the approaches it is trying out, but the likely long-run difficulties of taking this narrow route have to be articulated without compromising the admiration for what the Karzai government has achieved.

As for the global challenge of terrorism, we have reason to expect, from the world leaders working against it, rather greater clarity of thought than we are currently getting. The confusion generated by an implicit belief in the solitarist understanding of identity poses serious barriers to overcoming global terrorism and creating a world without ideologically organized large-scale violence. The recognition of multiple identities and of the world beyond religious affiliations, even for very religious people, can possibly make some difference in the troubled world in which we live.

Terrorism and Religion

I was privileged to know Daniel Pearl a little. He came to a talk of
mine in Paris in the summer of 2000, and we had a longish conversation afterward. He knew then that he was soon going to be
based in Bombay (or Mumbai, as it is now called), reporting for
the *Wall Street Journal* on the subcontinent. Later, early in February 2001, I saw him again in Bombay, and I had the opportunity
of continuing our conversation. I was struck not only by Pearl's
remarkable intelligence, but also by his commitment to pursue the
truth and, through that means, to help create a better—and less
unjust—world. We also discussed, particularly during our first
meeting, how violence in the world is often sown by ignorance and
confusion, as well as by injustices that receive little attention. I
was moved, intellectually as well as emotionally, by Daniel Pearl's
dedication to fight for peace and justice through the advancement
of understanding and enlightenment. It was that dedication to
investigate and explore that would ultimately cost him his life,
when the terrorists would capture and execute him in Pakistan the
year after I last met him.

Daniel's father, Judea Pearl, who is the president of the Daniel
Pearl Foundation, which is dedicated to intercultural understanding, recently expressed his frustration in a moving—and also
enlightening—article about the outcome of an important meeting
of Muslim scholars in Amman in Jordan. The conference, to
which 170 Islamic clerics and experts had come from forty countries, tried to define "the reality of Islam and its role in the contemporary society." The final communiqué of the Amman
conference, issued on July 6, 2005, stated categorically: "It is not
possible to declare as apostates any group of Muslims who
believes in Allah the Mighty and Sublime and His Messenger

(may Peace and Blessings be upon him) and the pillars of faith, and respects the pillars of Islam and does not deny any necessary article of religion."[14] Judea Pearl felt disappointed, though he is too gentle and tolerant to express anger, with the conclusion that "belief in basic tenets of faith provides an immutable protection from charges of apostasy." He points out that this implies that "bin Laden, Abu Musab al-Zarqawi and the murderers of Daniel Pearl and Nick Berg will remain bona fide members of the Muslim faith, as long as they do not explicitly renounce it."

Judea Pearl's disappointment reflected a hope he had clearly entertained that the horrible acts of terror would not only receive denunciation from Muslim scholars (which they, in fact, did, in no uncertain terms), but would also be a sufficient ground for religious excommunication. But no excommunication occurred, and given the way the demands of being a Muslim are foundationally defined in Islam, it could not have. In Judea Pearl's case, the personal disappointment is entirely natural, but when the same expectation is used in the strategy of fighting terrorism at the global level, it can legitimately be asked whether Western strategists have good reason to expect that a religion itself can be recruited to fight terrorism through declaring the terrorists to be apostates. That expectation was dashed in Amman, but was it a reasonable expectation for strategists to entertain?

As was discussed earlier, we have to ask whether it is at all possible to define a "true Muslim" in terms of beliefs about confrontation and tolerance, on which Islam does not dictate and on which different Muslims have taken widely different positions over many centuries. This freedom allowed, of course, King Abdullah II of Jordan to firmly assert, as he did during the very same conference, that "the acts of violence and terrorism carried out by certain extremist groups in the name of Islam are utterly contradictory to the principles and ideology of Islam." But that diagnosis and indeed reprimand—still does not take us to a position by which the persons thus criticized must be seen as "apostate," and it is that central point that the Amman declaration by Muslim scholars affirmed. Apostasy is a matter of basic religious belief and specified practice; it is not a matter of the correctness in interpreting social or political principles, or of the rightness of civil society, or even of identifying what most Muslims would see as terrible civil conduct or abominable political behavior.

Richness of Muslim Identities

If a Muslim person's only identity were that of being Islamic, then of course all moral and political judgments of the person would have to be specifically linked with religious assessment. It is that solitarist illusion that underlies the Western—particularly Anglo-American—attempt to recruit Islam in the so-called war against terrorism.[15] The unwillingness to distinguish between (1) a Muslim person's variety of associations and affiliations (these can vary widely from person to person) and (2) his or her Islamic identity in particular has tended to tempt Western leaders to fight political battles against terrorism through the exotic route of defining—or redefining—Islam. What needs to be recognized is not only that this solitarist approach has accomplished little so far, but also that it cannot really be expected to achieve much given the distinction between religious issues, on the one hand, and other matters on which Muslims, no matter how religious, have to take their own decisions. Even though the borderline between the two domains may be hard to delineate, the domain of religious excommunication and apostasy cannot be extended much beyond the well-established central tenets of Islamic canons and identified practice. Religion is not, and cannot be, a person's all-encompassing identity.[16]

It is, of course, true that the so-called Islamic terrorists have repeatedly tried to extend the role of religion very far into other spheres, contrary (as King Abdullah rightly noted) to the generally accepted principles and domain of Islam. It is also true that the recruiters for terrorism would like Muslims to forget that they have other identities too and that they have to decide on many important political and moral matters and take responsibility for their decisions, rather than being led by the recruiters' advocacy based on their uncommon reading of Islam. The mistaken presumptions involved in such efforts can certainly be scrutinized and criticized. But the strategy of trying to stop such recruitment by declaring the recruiters to be "apostate" would also—I fear in a somewhat singularist way—extend the reach of religion beyond its established domain.

The basic recognition of the multiplicity of identities would militate against trying to see people in exclusively religious terms, no matter how religious they are within the domain of religion. Attempts to tackle terrorism through the aid of religion has had the effect of magnifying in Britain and America the voice of Islamic clerics and other members of the religious establishment on matters that are not in the domain of religion, at a time when the political and social roles of Muslims in civil society, including in the practice of democracy, need emphasis and much greater support. What religious extremism has done to demote and downgrade the responsible political action of citizens (irrespective of religious ethnicity) has been, to some extent, reinforced, rather than eradicated, by the attempt to fight terrorism by trying to recruit the religious establishment on "the right side." In the downplaying of political and social identities as opposed to religious identity, it is civil society that has been the loser, precisely at a time when there is a great need to strengthen it.

CHAPTER 5

————————

WEST AND
ANTI-WEST

Resistance to "Westernization" has a strong presence in the world today. It can take the form of shunning ideas that are seen as "Western," even when these ideas have occurred and flourished historically in many non-Western societies and have been a part of our global past. There is, for example, nothing exclusively "Western" about valuing liberty or defending public reasoning. And yet their being labeled as "Western" can produce a negative attitude toward them in other societies. Indeed, this can be seen in different forms of anti-Western rhetoric, varying from the championing of "Asian values" (this flourished particularly in East Asia in the 1990s) to insisting that "Islamic ideals" must be deeply hostile to everything the West stands for (an attitude that has gained considerable ground in recent years).

Part of the reason for this fixation with the West, or the *alleged* West, lies in the history of colonialism. Western imperialism over the last few centuries not only subverted the political independence of the countries that were ruled or dominated by the colonial powers, it also created an attitudinal climate that is obsessed with the West, even though the form of that obsession may vary widely—from slavish imitation, on one side, to resolute hostility on the other. The dialectics of the colonized mind includes both admiration and disaffection.

It would be a mistake to try to see postcolonial disaffection toward the West as just a reaction to actual colonial maltreatment, exploitation, and humiliation. There is more to postcolonial alienation than a reaction to the real history of abuse. We have to go deeper than seeking an instant explanation through invoking a "tit for tat" reaction—more on this presently.

And yet it is also important to recognize and remember that serious abuses did occur, and sometimes the social memory—preserved in prose or in poetry—of those actual transgressions still animates anti-Western attitudes today. Now that a warm nostalgia for the empires of yesterday—for the British in particular—seems to be making something of a comeback in Europe (and oddly enough, even in America), it is worth remembering that the perceived sense of colonial iniquity was not entirely baseless.

In addition to the infringements and atrocities committed by the colonial masters (well illustrated by the notorious Amritsar massacre in India on the thirteenth of April 1919 when 379 unarmed people were gunned down at a peaceful meeting), their general psychological attitude toward the subject people often generated a strong sense of humiliation and an imposition of perceived inferiority. The role of colonial humiliation in the dialectics of dominated people deserves at least as much attention as the influence of economic and political asymmetry imposed by the imperial authorities.

In *Pilgrim's Progress*, John Bunyan talks about "the valley of humiliation." Bunyan knew humiliation well, having spent many years in prison. In fact, he began writing *Pilgrim's Progress* during his second bout in jail in the 1670s (the book was published in 1678). But harrowing as the image of that imagined valley is, it cannot begin to match the world of indignity and degradation that, say, Africa was already experiencing in Bunyan's seventeenth-century world. Africa, which gave birth to the human race and was responsible for many of the pioneering developments in the growth of world civilization, was beginning to be turned into a continent of European domination and the hunting ground for slaves to be transported like animals to the New World.

The devastating effects of humiliation on human lives can hardly be exaggerated. The historical ills of the slave trade and colonization (and the racial insults that were added to physical and social injury) have been seen as "the war against Africa" by the Independent Commission on Africa, chaired by Albert Tevoedjre, which identifies Africa's principal task today as "winning the war against humiliation" (the chosen title of the report).[1] As the commission argues, the subjugation and denigration of Africa over the last few centuries have left a massively negative legacy against which the people of the continent have to battle. That legacy includes not only the devastation of old institutions and the forgone opportunity to build new ones, but also the destruction of social confidence, on which so much else depends.

Similar undermining also occurred elsewhere. Now that the actual memory of the British Raj has largely faded in Britain and the nostalgia for it (along with a taste for curry) is quite strong, it is worth recollecting that the complex attitude of South Asians to Britain include reactions to some particularly unattractive components, which coexisted with other elements, of the imperial mind. There was never any dearth of Indophiles in the imperial hierarchy and they were particularly important in the eighteenth century.

But once the empire settled down, the need to keep some distance became a crucial part of the education of the British officer from early on in the nineteenth century.[2] One of the rationales for this was best explained in James Mill's famous history of India, which was a standard reading of the imperial cadres about to undertake the voyage to that country, to wit: while "our ancestors, though rough, were sincere," in contrast, "under the glosing exterior of the Hindu, lies a general disposition to deceit and perfidy."[3] The book, which Mill had written without visiting India even once and without being able to read any Indian language, was regarded as altogether authoritative by the British administration, and was described by Lord Macaulay, who would soon be the most powerful British administrator in India, as "on the whole the greatest historical work which has appeared in our language since that of Gibbon."[4]

In this "bible for the British Indian officer," Mill also made clear that while some had taken the Indians and the Hindus to be "a people of high civilization," he had determined that "they have in reality made but a few of the earliest steps in the progress to civilization."[5] To illustrate, let me briefly discuss one of the various denunciations that fill up Mill's pages, related to his assessment of classical Indian astronomy. It specifically concerns the arguments for a rotating earth and a model of gravitational attraction proposed by Aryabhata, who was born in A.D. 476—arguments that were also investigated by later Indian astronomers Varahamihira and Brahmagupta in the sixth and seventh centuries respectively. These works were well known in the Arab world and generated much discussion there. In fact, Brahmagupta's book was translated into Arabic in the eighth century and retranslated by the Iranian mathematician Alberuni in the eleventh (since Alberuni thought that the previous Arabic rendering was somewhat defective).

In the late eighteenth century, William Jones, serving in the East India Company in Calcutta, came to know about these old Sanskrit documents, and he expressed admiration for these early Indian astronomical works.[6] Commenting on this, Mill expressed total astonishment at Jones's gullibility.[7] After ridiculing the absurdity of this attribution and commenting on the "pretensions and interests" of Jones's Indian informants, Mill concluded that it was "extremely natural that Sir William Jones, whose pundits had become acquainted with the ideas of European philosophers respecting the system of the universe, should hear from them that those ideas were contained in their own books."[8] Thus, Mill's belief in the "general disposition to deceit and perfidy" of Indians ended up having an explanatory function in his history of India as well.

At the end of a comprehensive attack on supposed Indian achievements particularly in mathematics and science, Mill came to the conclusion that the Indian civilization was on a par with "other inferior ones" known to Mill: "very nearly the same with that of the Chinese, the Persians, and the Arabians," and just as inferior as those of other "subordinate nations, the Japanese, Cochinchinese, Siamese, Burmans, and even Malays and Tibetans."[9] After that comprehensive assessment, if these "subordinate nations" fell prey to some disaffection toward the colonizing West, it may be a little unfair to attribute it simply to self-generated paranoia.

Dialectics of the Colonized Mind

And yet the limited horizons of the colonized mind and its fixation with the West—whether in resentment or in admiration—has to be overcome. It cannot make sense to see oneself primarily as someone who (or whose ancestors) have been misrepresented, or treated badly, by colonialists, no matter how true that identification may be.

There are undoubtedly occasions when that diagnosis would be quite relevant. Given the continuation of some colonial asymmetries in different forms—the term "neocolonialism" is often used to refer to them—and the powerful new temptation to see great merit in past imperial arrangements, those occasions may well arise with some frequency. But to lead a life in which resentment against an imposed inferiority from past history comes to dominate one's priorities today cannot but be unfair to oneself. It can also vastly deflect attention from other objectives that those emerging from past colonies have reason to value and pursue in the contemporary world.

Indeed, the colonized mind is parasitically obsessed with the extraneous relation with the colonial powers. While the impact of such an obsession can take many different forms, that general dependency can hardly be a good basis for self-understanding. As I shall presently discuss, the nature of this "reactive self-perception" has had far-reaching effects on contemporary affairs. This includes (1) the encouragement it has given to needless hostility to many global ideas (such as democracy and personal liberty) under the mistaken impression that these are "Western" ideas, (2) the contribution it has made to a distorted reading of the intellectual and scientific history of the world (including what is quintessentially "Western" and what has mixed heritage), and (3) the support it has tended to give to the growth of religious fundamentalism and even to international terrorism.

This, I appreciate, is quite a list of direct and indirect contributions, but before I go into them more fully, let me illustrate the nature of this reactive self-perception with a historical example involving intellectual identity. It concerns the interpretation of

India's past and the self-perception of Indian identity.[10] The colonial undermining—like that by James Mill—of India's achievements in science and mathematics contributed to an "adapted" self-perception that chose "its own ground" for competition with the West, emphasizing India's comparative advantage in "spiritual" matters. Partha Chatterjee has discussed the emergence of this attitude:

> [A]nticolonial nationalism creates its own domain of sovereignty within colonial society well before its political battle with the imperial power. It does this by dividing the world of social institutions and practices into two domains—the material and the spiritual. The material is the domain of the "outside," of the economy and of statecraft, of science and technology, a domain where the West had proved its superiority and the East had succumbed. In this domain, then, Western superiority had to be acknowledged and its accomplishments carefully studied and replicated. The spiritual, on the other hand, is an "inner" domain bearing the "essential" marks of cultural identity. The greater one's success in imitating Western skills in the material domain, therefore, the greater the need to preserve the distinctiveness of one's spiritual culture. This formula is, I think, a fundamental feature of anticolonial nationalisms in Asia and Africa.[11]

It is possible that Chatterjee's insightful diagnosis is perhaps a little too "India-centered," and his geographically inclusive conclusion—covering "Asia and Africa"—may be too much of a generalization based on the nineteenth-century experience of the Indian subcontinent in particular. Reactive self-identities can indeed operate in many different ways in different regions and times. Nevertheless, it would be, I think, correct to accept that Chatterjee rightly identifies an important aspect of the propensity

that developed in many parts of European empires in Asia and
Africa, including the Indian subcontinent during the British rule.
It certainly encouraged Indians to put their "spiritual foot" forward. This was, to a considerable extent, a reaction to a rather dis-
missive imperial reading of India's analytical and scientific past
history.[12] This selective focus, while combative against the imperial claims of overall superiority (the spiritual ground was "ours,"
it was claimed), had the effect of neglecting—and downplaying—
a huge part of India's scientific and mathematical heritage.
Indeed, in this respect, it consolidated James Mill's misreading of
India's intellectual past, rather than resisting it.

There is also an example of a more general pattern of development of reactive identity. One of the oddities of the postcolonial
world is the way many non-Western people today tend to think of
themselves as quintessentially "the other," as Akeel Bilgrami, the
philosopher, has beautifully discussed in a paper called "What Is
a Muslim?"[13] They are led to define their identity primarily in terms
of being *different from* Western people. Something of this "other-
ness" can be seen in the emergence of various self-definitions that
characterize cultural or political nationalism, and even in the contribution this reactive view makes to fundamentalism.

While these "non-Western"—and sometimes "anti-Western"
—views involve an emphatic seeking of independence from colonial dominance, they are, in fact, thoroughly foreign-dependent—
in a negative and contrary form. The dialectics of the captivated
mind can lead to a deeply biased and parasitically reactive self-
perception. Also, this singular mode of thinking can take the form
of trying to "get even" with the West (as many terrorists see themselves as doing, with explicit or implicit references to atrocities
from the colonial period), and of seeking justice in the contemporary world by invoking the past and present offenses of the
Western world. It can also take the more positive form of wanting

to "catch up with the West," trying to "beat it at its own game," or attempting to build a society that "even the Westerners must admire." These positive programs may not have the contrariness and improvident anger of the corrective or retributive agenda, but they too make one's identity deeply subservient to relations with others. The colonial masters of yesterday continue to exert an enormous influence on the postcolonial mind today.

Another unfortunate consequence of viewing oneself as "the other" is that it tends to make the Western expropriation of the global heritage of universalist political ideas (such as the importance of liberty or of democratic reasoning) much more damaging. Misdiagnosis of what is "Western" (very common as it is, as was discussed in chapter 3) can take a heavy toll by undermining the support for democracy or liberty in the non-Western world. It can, in addition, help to undermine the understanding of objectivity in science and knowledge, on some alleged ground of the need to be adequately skeptical of "Western science."

The role colonized dialectics plays in making lives harder in Asia and Africa can be illustrated with different types of examples. To consider a particularly far-reaching illustration, Mamphela Ramphele, who is a remarkable combination of distinguished doctor, leading antiapartheid activist, and global policy maker, has insightfully discussed how, in the inadequate protection against the emergence of the AIDS epidemic in South Africa, the nature of public policy in postapartheid South Africa has been influenced by "the mistrust of science that has traditionally been controlled by white people." It added force to another dialectical influence in the direction of inaction arising from "the fear of acknowledging an epidemic that could easily be used to fan the worst racial stereotyping."[14]

The dialectics of the colonized mind can impose a heavy penalty on the lives and freedoms of people who are reactively obsessed with the West. It can wreak havoc on lives in other countries as well, when the reaction takes the violent form of seeking confrontation, including what is seen as retribution. I shall return to this distressing issue later on in this chapter.

Asian Values and Smaller Themes

One of the remarkable articulations of a reactive non-Western identity can be found in the championing of "Asian values" which have come from many East Asian exponents. This is in reaction, to a great extent, to the Western claim to be the historical depository of ideas on liberty and rights (Samuel Huntington's claims in that line were discussed earlier). Proponents of the excellence of "Asian values" do not dispute this claim, indeed quite the contrary. Instead it is argued that while Europe may have been the home ground of liberty and individual rights, "Asian values" cherish discipline and order, and this, it is alleged, is a marvelous priority. It tells the West that it can keep its individual liberties and rights but Asia will do better with its adherence to orderly conduct and disciplined behavior. The West-obsessed form of this grand "Asian" claim is hard to miss.

The glorification of "Asian values" has typically flourished best in countries to the east of Thailand (particularly among political leaders and government spokesmen), even though there is a still more ambitious claim that the rest of Asia is also rather "similar." For example, the formidable senior minister (and former prime minister) of Singapore, Lee Kuan Yew, who is one of the great architects of East Asian resurgence and a visionary political leader in his own right, outlined "the fundamental difference between Western concepts of society and government and East Asian concepts" by explaining, "[W]hen I say East Asians, I mean Korea, Japan, China, Vietnam, as distinct from Southeast Asia, which is a mix between the Sinic and the Indian, though Indian culture itself emphasizes similar values."[15] Lee Kuan Yew went on to link the emphasis on Asian values to the need to resist the hegemony of the West, in particular the political dominance of the United States, pointing out that Singapore is "not a client state of America."[16]

Cultural and value differences between Asia and the West were stressed by several official delegations at the World Conference on Human Rights in Vienna in 1993. The foreign minister of Singapore warned that "universal recognition of the ideal of human rights can be harmful if universalism is used to deny or mask the reality of diversity."[17] The Chinese delegation played a leading role in emphasizing regional differences, and in making sure that the prescriptive framework adopted in the declarations made room for "regional diversity." The Chinese foreign minister even put on record the proposition that the Asian priorities demand that "individuals must put the states' rights before their own."[18]

I have already discussed, in chapter 3, why this cultural diagnosis is so difficult to sustain. Support for ideas of liberty and public discussion, and what may be called basic human rights, have been articulated no less often in Asia—in India, China, Japan, and in various other countries in East, Southeast, South, and West Asia—than in Europe.[19] The point to note here is not just the debatable nature of the diagnosis of "Asian values" and the fact that it seriously underestimates the range and reach of the intellectual heritage of Asia. It is also important, in the context of the present analysis, to see the thoroughly reactive nature of the genesis of this view. The need to differentiate from the West is clearly visible in this postcolonial dialectic, and it is also easy to see the attraction for many Asians of the claim that Asia has something much better than Europe.

As it happens, Lee Kuan Yew's own claims to special distinction would be hard to deny. Even though Asian advocates of political liberty and democracy, which include the present author, cannot but be frustrated that Lee's words and deeds have run in the opposite direction to ours, it would be wrong to withhold credit where it is due. There is, in particular, the need to recognize that Lee Kuan Yew's Singapore not only has been economically very successful, but has also been able to give its minority communities a strong sense of belonging, security, and a shared national identity in a way that most European countries with sizable minorities have not been able to provide for their own minority communities. One could not help thinking about the contrast as the urban riots, linked with race and ethnicity, erupted in France in the fall of 2005.

And yet the fact remains that Lee's generalization about values in Asia is hard to vindicate on the basis of an unbiased reading of Asian historical classics as well as contemporary experiences and writings in Asia. The diagnosis of Asian values in the thesis of Lee and others is clearly influenced by a reactive mode of responding to Western claims of being the natural home of liberty and rights. Rather than challenging that claim, Lee proposes to turn the tables on the West by arguing: Yes, we don't do much for Western ideas of liberty and rights, for we have something better. This version of anti-Western rhetoric is also, in a dialectical sense, obsessed with the West.

Colonialism and Africa

Perhaps the most troubled continent in the last century, particularly in the second half of it, has been Africa. Toward the middle of the century the formal ending of empires—British, French, Portuguese, and Belgian—came with a strong promise of democratic developments in Africa. Instead the bulk of the region soon fell prey to authoritarianism and militarism, a breakdown of civil order and educational and health services, and a veritable explosion of local conflicts, intercommunity strife, and civil wars.

This is not the occasion to go into an investigation of the causal story behind these discouraging developments, from which Africa is only now beginning to pull away, even though the task is made harder by the massive problem of epidemics, new (such as AIDS) and old (such as malaria), which is blighting many parts of the continent. I have tried to comment on these complex developments elsewhere (particularly in my book *Development as Freedom*),[20] and will confine myself here only to a couple of comments that relate in particular to the continued role of colonialism and the functioning of the captivated mind.

First, even though much has been written about the possible effects of Western domination in the world in hindering growth and development of the African economies (for example, through artificially imposed limits on export markets in Europe and America, of agricultural products, textiles and other commodities, and the unbearable burden of debts, which is only now beginning to get relieved), it is also important to see the role of Western powers in the recent history of political and military developments in the continent.

Africa's misfortunes in the period of classic imperialism was followed, as it happens, by another period of institutional handicap during the cold war in the second half of the twentieth century. The cold war, which was substantially fought on African soil (though this is rarely acknowledged), made each of the superpowers cultivate military rulers friendly to itself and, perhaps more importantly, hostile to the enemy. When military overlords such as Mobuto Sese Seko of Congo, or Jonas Savimbi of Angola, or whoever, busted social and political orders (and ultimately economic order too) in Africa, they could rely on support either from the Soviet Union or from the United States and its allies, depending on their military alliances. A military usurper of civilian authority never lacked a superpower friend, linked through a military alliance. A continent that seemed in the 1950s to be poised to develop active democratic politics was soon being run by an assortment of dictatorial strongmen who were linked to one side or the other in the militancy of the cold war. They competed in despotism with apartheid-based South Africa.

That picture is slowly changing now, with postapartheid South Africa playing a leading part in the constructive change. However, the West's military presence in—and incitement to—Africa has increasingly taken a different form, to wit, that of being the principal supplier of the arms sold globally, which are frequently used to sustain local wars and military conflicts, and which have very destructive consequences, not least on the economic prospects of poor countries. Even though the selling—and "pushing"—of arms is obviously not the only issue to be addressed in reducing the military conflicts in the continent (the demand side of the arms market reflects, of course, problems within the region), the need for curbing the massive international trade in arms is extremely strong right now. Armament is a business for which the selling of arms has typically been quite close to the pushing of the hardware.

The principal suppliers of armament in the world market today are the G8 countries, which were responsible for 84 percent of the arms sold in the period between 1998 and 2003.[21] Japan, the only non-Western country among the G8, is also the only one among them that abstains from this trade. The United States alone was responsible for about half of the arms sold in the world market, with two-thirds of its exports going to developing countries, including Africa. The arms are used not only with bloody results, but also with devastating effects on the economy, the polity, and the society. In some respects, this is a continuation of the unhelpful role of world powers in the development of political militarism in Africa during the sixties through the eighties, when the cold war was fought out over Africa. The world powers bear an awesome responsibility for contributing, in the cold-war years, to the subversion of democracy in Africa. The selling and pushing of arms gives them a continuing role in the escalation of military conflicts today—in Africa and elsewhere. The U.S. refusal to agree to a joint crackdown even on illicit exports of small arms (a very modest proposal put forward by Kofi Annan a few years ago) illustrates the difficulties involved.

Among the adversities Africa faces today in trying to move away from its colonial history and the cold-war suppression of democracy is the continuation of the successor phenomenon in the form of militarism and continued warfare, in which the West has a facilitating role. In the civilizational categorization, much used these days, the West may frequently be glorified as having "a tradition of individual rights and liberties unique among civilized societies" (to invoke Huntington's phrase), but aside from seeing the historical limitations of that thesis (discussed earlier), it is also important to take note of the role of the West in the undermining of "individual rights and liberties" in *other* countries, including those in Africa. Western governments need to undertake policy changes that would restrict or halt the merchants of death from within their borders. Decolonizing the colonized mind must be supplemented by changes in Western international policy.

Second, there are, of course, a lot of problems in the mind too. As Kwame Anthony Appiah has argued, "[I]deological decolonisation is bound to fail if it neglects either endogenous 'tradition' or exogenous 'Western' ideas."[22] In particular, the often repeated argument that democracy does not suit Africa—

it is a "very Western thing"—has had an enormously negative effect in weakening the defense of democracy in Africa from the 1960s to the 1980s. Aside from the need to see the constructive role of democracy in Africa (as in other parts of the world), the cultural argument is doubly defective both because a Western invention could still be very useful in other parts of the world (penicillin is an obvious example) and because there is, in fact, a long tradition, discussed earlier, of participatory governance in Africa as well.

Meyer Fortes and Edward Evans-Pritchard, the great anthropologists of Africa, argued in their classic book *African Political Systems,* published more than sixty years ago, that "the structure of an African state implies that kings and chiefs rule by consent."[23] There may have been some overgeneralization in this, as critics have argued, but there can be little doubt about the important role and continuing relevance of accountability and participation in the African political heritage. To overlook all that in trying to see the fight for democracy in Africa only as an attempt to import the "Western idea" of democracy from abroad would be (as was discussed earlier) a profound misdescription.

Here again the understanding of a plurality of commitments and appreciation of the coexistence of multiple identities are extremely important, and it is especially so in the decolonization of Africa. Appiah explains how influenced he was by his own father's "multiple attachment to his identities: above all as an Asante, as a Ghanian, as an African, and as a Christian and a Methodist."[24] A proper understanding of the world of plural identities requires clarity of thinking about the recognition of our multiple commitments and affiliations, even though this may tend to be drowned by the flood of unifocal advocacy of just one perspective or another. Decolonization of the mind demands a firm departure from the temptation of solitary identities and priorities.

Fundamentalism and the Centrality of the West

I turn now to fundamentalism, which has a remarkable presence in the contemporary world, and which plays a significant role in generating both loyalty and social disaffection. Fundamentalism, it must of course be noted, flourishes in the West as well as outside it. In fact, Darwin and evolutionary science seem to face bigger and more organized opposition today from the educated public in parts of America than almost anywhere else in the world. However, I shall concentrate here specifically on non-Christian fundamentalism, the connection of which with the colonial history of the world is important to understand.

The intensely anti-Western nature of some of the non-Christian fundamentalist movements in the world may make it implausible to suggest that they are, in fact, deeply dependent on the West. But they clearly have this dependency, especially to the extent that they focus on advancing values and priorities that are aimed explicitly and single-mindedly against Western conceptions and interests. Seeing oneself as "the other" (to invoke a telling concept well discussed by Akeel Bilgrami), in contrast with some external—in this case colonial—power structure, is part of the underlying belief system of some of the most sharply anti-Western fundamentalist movements, including the more fervent versions of Islamic fundamentalism.

In the days when Muslim rulers controlled the central terrain of the Old World and had massive command over it (between the seventh and seventeenth centuries), Muslims did not define their cultures and priorities in principally reactive terms. Even though the spread of Islam involved overcoming the hold of other religions—Christianity, Hinduism, Buddhism, and others— there was no need for Muslims to define themselves as "the other," in contrast with some dominant power in the world. There is something of a departure from that self-reliant perspective when the insistence on a unified anti-Western stand and the overwhelming commitment to fight the West—as the embodiment of the "Great Satan" or whatever—places the West at the center of the political stage of a fundamentalist viewpoint. There was no need for such a reactive self-definition in the grand days of Muslim preeminence.

To be sure, there is not much "need" for it today either. Being a Muslim involves positive religious beliefs (in particular, accepting that "there is no God but God" and that "Muhammad is the Messenger of God") and some duties of performance (like prayers). But within the broad requirements of these religious beliefs and performances, different Muslims can choose different views on secular subjects and decide on how to conduct their lives. And the vast majority of Muslims across the world do just that even today. In contrast, some of the Islamic fundamentalist movements carve out for themselves a particular territory which involves a social vision and a political outlook in which the West has a powerfully negative but central role.[25]

If contemporary Islamic fundamentalism is, in this sense, parasitic on the West, the terrorism aimed at America or Europe that sometimes goes with it is even more so. To dedicate one's life to undermining the West and to blowing up prominent edifices that have practical or symbolic importance in the West reflects an obsession with the West that overwhelms all other priorities and values. It is one of the preoccupations that can be much encouraged by the dialectics of the colonized mind.

In crude civilizational classifications, one of the distinctions that is greatly blurred, as was discussed in chapter 4, is that between (1) a person's being a Muslim, which is an important identity but not necessarily his or her only identity, and (2) a person's being wholly or primarily defined by his or her Islamic identity. The blurring, which is widely seen in discussions of contemporary politics, of the distinction between being a Muslim and having a singular Islamic identity is driven by a number of confusing concerns, of which an exclusive reliance on crude civilizational categories is certainly one. However, the emergence of reactive self-conceptions in anti-Western thought and rhetoric also contributes to this conceptual clouding. Culture, literature, science, and mathematics are more easily shared than religion. The tendency to see themselves as "the other," sharply distinguished from the West, has the effect of making many people in Asia and Africa place much greater emphasis on their dedicated *non*-Western identities—distanced from the Judeo-Christian heritage of the West—than on other parts of their self-understanding.

I shall have to come back to this general classificatory question for further consideration, including its role in disorienting some of the responses to fundamentalism and terrorism that have been undertaken in America and Europe.

CHAPTER 6

CULTURE AND CAPTIVITY

T he world has come to the conclusion—more defiantly than
should have been needed—that culture matters. The world
is obviously right—culture does matter. However, the real question is: "*How* does culture matter?"[1] The confining of culture into
stark and separated boxes of civilizations or of religious identities,
discussed in the last two chapters, takes too narrow a view of cultural attributes. Other cultural generalizations, for example,
about national, ethnic, or racial groups, can also present astonishingly limited and bleak understandings of the characteristics of
the human beings involved. When a hazy perception of culture is
combined with fatalism about the dominating power of culture,
we are, in effect, asked to be imaginary slaves of an illusory force.

And yet simple cultural generalizations have great effectiveness
in fixing our way of thinking. The fact that such generalizations
abound in popular convictions and in informal communication is

easily recognized. Not only are the implicit and twisted beliefs frequently the subject matter of racist jokes and ethnic slurs, they sometimes surface as grand theories. When there is an accidental correlation between cultural prejudice and social observation (no matter how casual), a theory is born, and it may refuse to die even after the chance correlation has vanished without a trace.

Consider the labored jokes against the Irish (such crudities as "How many Irishmen do you need to change a lightbulb?"), which have had some currency in England for a long time, and which are similar to equally silly jokes about the Poles in America. These crudities had the superficial appearance of fitting well with the depressing predicament of the Irish economy, when the Irish economy was doing quite badly. But when the Irish economy started growing astonishingly rapidly—indeed in recent years faster than any other European economy (Ireland is now richer in per capita income than nearly every country in Europe)—the cultural stereotyping and its allegedly profound economic and social relevance were not junked as sheer and unmitigated rubbish. Theories have lives of their own, quite defiantly of the phenomenal world that can actually be observed.

Imagined Truths and Real Policies

Such theories are, often enough, not just harmless fun. For example, cultural prejudice did play a role in the treatment Ireland received from the British government, and had a part even in the nonprevention of the famines of the 1840s. Among the influences that had an effect on London's treatment of Irish economic problems, cultural alienation did count. While poverty in Britain was typically attributed to economic change and fluctuations, Irish poverty was widely viewed in England (as Richard Ned Lebow, the political analyst, has argued) as being caused by laziness, indifference, and ineptitude, so that "Britain's mission" was not seen as one "to alleviate Irish distress but to civilize her people and to lead them to feel and act like human beings."[2]

The search for cultural causes of Ireland's economic predicament extends far back, at least to the sixteenth century, well reflected in Edmund Spenser's *The Faerie Queene*, published in 1590. The art of blaming the victims, plentifully present in *The Faerie Queene* itself, was put to effective use during the famines of the 1840s, and new elements were added to the old narrative. For example, the Irish taste for potatoes was added to the list of calamities which the natives had, in the English view, brought on themselves. Charles Edward Trevelyan, the head of the Treasury during the famines, expressed his belief that London had done all that could be done for Ireland, even though the famine killed rampantly (in fact, the mortality rate was higher in the Irish famines than in any other recorded famine anywhere in the world).

Trevelyan also proposed a rather remarkable cultural exegesis of Ireland's manifest hunger by linking it with the allegedly limited horizons of Irish culture (in contrast with putting any blame on British governance): "There is scarcely a woman of the peasant class in the West of Ireland whose culinary art exceeds the boiling of a potato."[3] The remark can be seen as an encouraging departure from the English hesitation about making international criticism of culinary art elsewhere (the French, the Italian, and the Chinese may be next). But the oddity of that cultural explanation of Irish hunger certainly merits a place in the annals of eccentric anthropology.

The connection between cultural bigotry and political tyranny can be very close. The asymmetry of power between the ruler and the ruled, which generates a heightened sense of identity contrast,

can be combined with cultural prejudice in explaining away failures of governance and public policy. Winston Churchill made the
famous remark that the Bengal famine of 1943, which occurred
just before India's independence from Britain in 1947 (it would
also prove to be the last famine in India in the century, since
famines disappeared with the Raj), was caused by the tendency
of people there to "breed like rabbits." The explication belongs to
the general tradition of finding explanations of disasters not in bad
administration, but in the culture of the subjects, and this habit
of thought had some real influence in crucially delaying famine
relief in the Bengal famine, which killed between two and three
million people. Churchill rounded things up by expressing his
frustration that the job of governing India was made so difficult
by the fact that the Indians were "the beastliest people in the
world, next to the Germans."[4] Cultural theories evidently have
their uses.

Korea and Ghana

Cultural explanations of economic underdevelopment have
recently been given much ground. Consider, for example, the following argument from the influential and engaging book jointly
edited by Lawrence Harrison and Samuel Huntington called *Culture Matters;* it occurs in Huntington's introductory essay, called
"Cultures Count," in that volume:

> In the early 1990s, I happened to come across economic data on
> Ghana and South Korea in the early 1960s, and I was astonished
> to see how similar their economies were then. . . . Thirty years
> later, South Korea had become an industrial giant with the four-

teenth largest economy in the world, multinational corporations, major exports of automobiles, electronic equipment, and other sophisticated manufactures, and per capita income approximately that of Greece. Moreover it was on its way to the consolidation of democratic institutions. No such changes had occurred in Ghana, whose per capita income was now about one-fifteenth that of South Korea's. How could this extraordinary difference in development be explained? Undoubtedly, many factors played a role, but it seemed to me that culture had to be a large part of the explanation. South Koreans valued thrift, investment, hard work, education, organization, and discipline. Ghanians had different values. In short, cultures count.[5]

There may well be something of interest in this way-out comparison (perhaps even a quarter-truth torn out of context), but the contrast does call for probing examination. As used in the explanation just cited, the causal story is extremely deceptive. There were many important differences—other than their cultural predispositions—between Ghana and Korea in the 1960s.

First, the class structures in the two countries were quite different, with a much bigger—and proactive—role for the business classes in South Korea. Second, the politics were very different too, with the government in South Korea willing and eager to play a prime-moving role in initiating business-centered economic development in a way that was not true in Ghana. Third, the close relationship between the Korean economy and Japan, on the one hand, and the United States, on the other, made a big difference, at least in the early stages of Korean economic expansion.

Fourth—and perhaps most important—by the 1960s South Korea had acquired a much higher literacy rate and a much more expanded school system than Ghana had. Korean progress in school education had been largely brought about in the post-

Second World War period, mainly through resolute public policy, and it could not be seen just as a reflection of culture (except in the general sense in which culture is seen to include everything happening in a country).[6] On the basis of the slender scrutiny that backed Huntington's conclusion, it is hard to justify either the cultural triumphalism in favor of Korean culture or the radical pessimism about Ghana's future to which Huntington is led through his reliance on cultural determinism.

This is not to suggest that cultural factors are irrelevant to the process of development. But they do not work in isolation from social, political, and economic influences. Nor are they immutable. If cultural issues are taken into account, among others, in a fuller accounting of societal change, they can greatly help to broaden our understanding of the world, including the process of development and the nature of our identity. While it is not particularly illuminating, nor especially helpful, to throw up one's hands in disapproval when faced with allegedly fixed cultural priorities ("Ghanians had different values," as Huntington puts it), it is useful to examine how values and behavior can respond to social change, for example, through the influence of schools and colleges. Let me refer again to South Korea, which was a much more literate and more educated society than Ghana in the 1960s (when the two economies appeared rather similar to Huntington). The contrast, as has already been mentioned, was substantially the result of public policies pursued in South Korea in the post–Second World War period. But the postwar public policies on education were also influenced by antecedent cultural features. Once we dissociate culture from the illusion of destiny, it can help to provide a better understanding of social change when placed together with other influences and interactive social processes.

In a two-way relationship, just as education influences culture, so can antecedent culture have an effect on educational policies. It is, for example, remarkable that nearly every country in the world with a powerful presence of Buddhist tradition has tended to embrace widespread schooling and literacy with some eagerness. This applies not only to Japan and Korea, but also to China, Thailand, Sri Lanka, and even to the otherwise retrograde Burma (Myanmar). The focus on enlightenment in Buddhism (the word "Buddha" itself means "enlightened") and the priority given to reading texts, rather than leaving it to the priests, can help to encourage educational expansion. Seen in a broader framework, there is probably something here to investigate and learn from.

It is, however, important also to see the interactive nature of the process in which contact with other countries and the knowledge of their experiences can make a big practical difference. There is every evidence that when Korea decided to move briskly forward in expanding school education at the end of the Second World War, it was influenced not just by its cultural interest in education, but also by a new understanding of the role and significance of education, based on the experiences of Japan and the West, including the United States.

Japanese Experience and Public Policy

There is a similar story, earlier on, of international interaction and national response in Japan's own history of educational development. When Japan emerged from its self-imposed isolation from the world (lasting since the seventeenth century, under the Tokugawa regime), it already had a relatively well-developed school system, and in this achievement Japan's traditional interest in education had played a significant part. Indeed, at the time of the Meiji restoration in 1868, Japan had a higher rate of literacy than Europe. And yet the rate of literacy in Japan was still low (as it obviously was in Europe too), and perhaps most importantly, the Japanese education system was quite out of touch with advances in science and technical knowledge in the industrializing West.

When, in 1852, Commodore Matthew Perry chugged into Edo Bay, puffing black smoke from the newly designed steamship, the Japanese were not only impressed—and somewhat terrified—and driven to accept diplomatic and trade relations with the United States, but they also had to reexamine and reassess their intellectual isolation from the world. This contributed to the political process that led to the Meiji restoration, and along with that came a determination to change the face of Japanese education. In the so-called Charter Oath, proclaimed in 1868, there is a firm declaration on the need to "seek knowledge widely throughout the world."[7]

The Fundamental Code of Education issued three years later, in 1872, put the new educational determination in unequivocal terms:

> There shall, in the future, be no community with an illiterate family, nor a family with an illiterate person.[8]

Kido Takayoshi, one of the most influential leaders of that period, put the basic issue with great clarity:

> Our people are no different from the Americans or Europeans of today; it is all a matter of education or lack of education.[9]

That was the challenge Japan took on with determination in the late nineteenth century.

Between 1906 and 1911, education consumed as much as 43 percent of the budgets of the towns and villages for Japan as a whole.[10] By 1906, the recruiting army officers found that, in contrast with the late nineteenth century, there was hardly any new recruit who was not already literate. By 1910, Japan had, it is generally acknowledged, universal attendance in primary schools. By 1913, even though Japan was still economically very poor and underdeveloped, it had become one of the largest producers of books in the world, publishing more books than Britain and indeed more than twice as many as the United States. Indeed, Japan's entire experience of economic development was, to a great extent, driven by human-capability formation, which included the role of education and training, and this was promoted *both* by public policy and by a supportive cultural climate (interacting with each other). The dynamics of associative relations are extraordinarily important in understanding how Japan laid the foundations of its spectacular economic and social development.

To carry the story further, Japan was not only a learner but also a great teacher. Development efforts of countries in East and Southeast Asia were profoundly influenced by Japan's experience in expanding education and its manifest success in transforming society and the economy. The so-called East Asian miracle was, to no small extent, an achievement inspired by the Japanese experience.

Paying attention to cultural interrelations, within a broad framework, can be a useful way of advancing our understanding of development and change. It would differ both from neglecting culture altogether (as some narrowly economic models do) and from the privileging of culture as an independent and stationary force, with an immutable presence and irresistible impact (as some cultural theorists seem to prefer). The illusion of cultural destiny is not only misleading, it can also be significantly debilitating, since it can generate a sense of fatalism and resignation among people who are unfavorably placed.

Culture in a Broad Framework

There can be little doubt that our cultural background can have quite a major influence on our behavior and thinking. Also, the quality of life we enjoy cannot but be influenced by our cultural background. It certainly can also influence our sense of identity and our perception of affiliation with groups of which we see ourselves as members. The skepticism I have been expressing here is not about the recognition of the basic importance of culture in human perception and behavior. It is about the way culture is sometimes seen, rather arbitrarily, as the central, inexorable, and entirely independent determinant of societal predicaments.

Our cultural identities can be extremely important, but they do not stand starkly alone and aloof from other influences on our understanding and priorities. There are a number of qualifications that have to be made while acknowledging the influence of culture on human lives and actions. First, important as culture is, it is not uniquely significant in determining our lives and identities. Other things, such as class, race, gender, profession, politics, also matter, and can matter powerfully.

Second, culture is not a homogeneous attribute—there can be great variations even within the same general cultural milieu. For example, contemporary Iran has both conservative ayatollahs and radical dissidents, just as America has room both for born-again Christians and for ardent nonbelievers (among a great many other schools of thought and behavior). Cultural determinists often underestimate the extent of heterogeneity within what is taken to be "one" culture. Discordant voices are often "internal," rather than coming from the outside. Also, depending on the particular aspect of culture we decide to concentrate on (for example, whether we focus on religion, or on literature, or on music), we can get quite a varying picture of the internal and external relations involved.

Third, culture does not sit still. The brief recollection of the educational transformation of Japan and Korea, with profound cultural implications, illustrated the importance of change, linked—as it often is—with public discussion and policy. Any presumption of stationariness—explicit or implicit—can be disastrously deceptive. The temptation toward using cultural determinism often takes the hopeless form of trying to moor the cultural anchor on a rapidly moving boat.

Fourth, culture interacts with other determinants of social perception and action. For example, economic globalization brings in not only more trade, but also more global music and cinema. Culture cannot be seen as an isolated force independent of other influences. The presumption of insularity—often implicitly invoked—can be deeply delusive.

Finally, we have to distinguish between the idea of *cultural liberty,* which focuses on our freedom either to preserve or to change our priorities (on the basis of greater knowledge or further reflection, or, for that matter, on the basis of our assessment of changing customs and fashions), and that of *valuing cultural conservation,* which has become a big issue in the rhetoric of multiculturalism (often providing support for the continuation of traditional lifestyles by new immigrants in the West). There is undoubtedly a strong case for including cultural freedom among the human capabilities people have reason to value, but there is a need also for a probing examination of the exact relation between cultural liberty and the priorities of multiculturalism.[11]

Multiculturalism and Cultural Freedom

In recent years, multiculturalism has gained much ground as an important value, or more accurately as a powerful slogan (since its underlying values are not altogether clear). The simultaneous flourishing of different cultures within the same country or region can be seen to be of importance on its own, but very often multi-culturalism is advocated on the ground that this is what cultural freedom demands. That claim has to be scrutinized further.

The importance of cultural freedom has to be distinguished from the celebration of every form of cultural inheritance, irre-spective of whether the persons involved would choose those particular practices given the opportunity of critical scrutiny and an adequate knowledge of other options and of the choices that actually exist. Even though there has been much discussion in recent years about the important and extensive role of cultural factors in social living and human development, the focus has often tended to be, explicitly or by implication, on the need for cultural conservation (for example, continued adherence to the conservative lifestyles of people whose geographical move to Europe or America is not always matched by cultural adapta-tion). Cultural freedom may include, among other priorities, the liberty to question the automatic endorsement of past traditions, when people—particularly young people—see a reason for changing their ways of living.

If freedom of human decision is important, then the results of a reasoned exercise of that freedom have to be valued, rather than being negated by an imposed precedence of unquestioned con-servation. The critical link includes our ability to consider alter-native options, to understand what choices are involved, and then to decide what we have reason to want.

It must, of course, be recognized that cultural liberty could be hampered when a society does not allow a particular community to pursue some traditional lifestyle that members of that community would freely choose to follow. Indeed, social suppression of particular lifestyles—of gays, of immigrants, of specific religious groups—is common in many countries in the world. The insistence that gays or lesbians live like heterosexuals, or stay inside closets, is not only a demand for uniformity, it is also a denial of the freedom of choice. If diversity is not allowed, then many choices would be rendered unviable. The allowing of diversity can indeed be important for cultural freedom.

Cultural diversity may be enhanced if individuals are allowed and encouraged to live as they would value living (instead of being restrained by ongoing tradition). For example, the freedom to pursue ethnically diverse lifestyles, for example, in food habits or in music, can make a society more culturally diverse precisely as a result of the exercise of cultural liberty. In this case, the importance of cultural diversity—instrumental as it is—will follow directly from the value of cultural liberty, since the former will be a consequence of the latter.

Diversity can also play a positive role in enhancing the freedom even of those who are not directly involved. For example, a culturally diverse society can bring benefits to others in the form of the ample variety of experiences which they are, as a consequence, in a position to enjoy. To illustrate, it can plausibly be argued that the rich tradition of African-American music—with its African lineage and American evolution—has not only helped to enhance the cultural freedom and self-respect of African-Americans, it has also expanded the cultural options of all people (African-American or not) and enriched the cultural landscape of America, and indeed the world.

Nevertheless, if our focus is on *freedom* (including cultural freedom), the significance of cultural diversity cannot be unconditional and must vary contingently with its causal connections with human freedom and its role in helping people to take their own decisions. In fact, the relation between cultural liberty and cultural diversity need not be uniformly positive. For example, the simplest way of having cultural diversity may, in some circumstances, be a total continuation of all the preexisting culture practices that *happen* to be present at a point in time (for example, new immigrants may be induced to continue their old, fixed ways and mores, and discouraged—directly or indirectly—from changing their behavior pattern at all). Does this suggest that for the sake of *cultural diversity* we should support *cultural conservatism* and ask people to stick to their own cultural background and not try to consider moving to other lifestyles even if they find good reasons to do so? The undermining of choice that this would involve would immediately deliver us to an antifreedom position, which would look for ways and means of blocking the choice of a changed living mode that many people may wish to have.

For example, young women from conservative immigrant families in the West might be kept on a short leash by the elders for fear that they would emulate the freer lifestyle of the majority community. Diversity will then be achieved at the cost of cultural liberty. If what is ultimately important is cultural freedom, then the valuing of cultural diversity must take a contingent and conditional form. The merit of diversity must thus depend on precisely *how* that diversity is brought about and sustained.

Indeed, to plead for cultural diversity on the ground that this is what the different groups of people have *inherited* is clearly not an argument based on cultural liberty (even though the case is sometimes presented *as if* it were a "profreedom" argument). Being born in a particular culture is obviously not an exercise of cultural liberty, and the preservation of something with which a person is stamped, simply because of birth, can hardly be, in itself, an exercise of freedom. Nothing can be justified in the name of freedom without actually giving people an opportunity for the exercise of that freedom, or at least without carefully assessing how an opportunity of choice would be exercised if it were available. Just as social suppression can be a denial of cultural freedom, the violation of freedom can also come from the tyranny of conformism that may make it difficult for members of a community to opt for other styles of living.

Schools, Reasoning, and Faith

Unfreedom can result also from a lack of knowledge and understanding of other cultures and of alternative lifestyles. To illustrate the main issue that is involved here, even an admirer (as this writer is) of the cultural freedoms that modern Britain has, by and large, succeeded in giving to people of different backgrounds and origins who are resident in that country can well have considerable misgivings about the official move in the United Kingdom toward extension of state-supported faith-based schools (as was briefly mentioned in the first chapter).

Rather than reducing existing state-financed faith-based schools, actually *adding* others to them—Muslim schools, Hindu schools, and Sikh schools to preexisting Christian ones—can have the effect of reducing the role of reasoning which the children may have the opportunity to cultivate and use. And this is happening at a time when there is a great need for broadening the horizon of understanding of other people and other groups, and when the ability to undertake reasoned decision-making is of particular importance. The limitations imposed on the children are especially acute when the new religious schools give children rather little opportunity to cultivate reasoned choice in determining the priorities of their lives. Also, they often fail to alert students to the need to decide for themselves how the various components of their identities (related respectively to nationality, language, literature, religion, ethnicity, cultural history, scientific interests, etc.) should receive attention.

This is not to suggest that the problems of bias (and the deliberate fostering of a blinkered vision) in these new faith-based British schools are anything as extreme as in, say, the fundamentalist madrasas in Pakistan, which have become a part of the breeding ground for intolerance and violence—and often for terrorism—in that strained part of the world. But the opportunity of cultivating reason and the recognition of the need for scrutinized choice can still be far less in these new faith-based schools, even in Britain, than in the more mixed and less sequestered places of learning in that country. The actual opportunities are often rather less than even in traditional religious schools—particularly in those Christian schools which have had a long tradition of having a broad curriculum, along with tolerating considerable skepticism about religious education itself (though these older schools too can be made considerably less restrictive than they already are).

The move toward faith-based schools in Britain reflects also a particular vision of Britain as "a federation of communities," rather than as a collectivity of human beings living in Britain, with diverse differences, of which religious and community-based distinctions constitute only one part (along with differences in language, literature, politics, class, gender, location, and other characteristics). It is unfair to children who have not yet had much opportunity of reasoning and choice to be put into rigid boxes guided by one specific criterion of categorization, and to be told: "That is your identity and this is all you are going to get."

In the annual lecture for 2001 at the British Academy which I had the privilege of giving (it was called "Other People"), I presented the argument that this "federational" approach has a great many problems, and in particular tends to reduce the development of human capabilities of British children from immigrant families in a significant way.[12] Since then the incidents of suicide bombing in London (in July 2005), carried out by British-born but deeply alienated young men, have added another dimension to the question of self-perception and its cultivation in Britain. However, I would argue that the basic limitation of the federationist approach goes well beyond any possible connection with terrorism. There is an important need not only to discuss the relevance of our common humanity—a subject on which schools can play (and have often played in the past) a critical role. There is, in addition, the important recognition that human identities can take many distinct forms and that people have to use reasoning to decide on how to see themselves, and what significance they should attach to having been born a member of a particular community. I shall have the opportunity to return to this issue in the last two chapters of the book.

The importance of nonsectarian and nonparochial school education that expands, rather than reduces, the reach of reasoning (including critical scrutiny) would be hard to exaggerate. Shakespeare gave voice to the concern that "some are born great, some achieve greatness, and some have greatness thrust upon them." In the schooling of children, it is necessary to make sure that *smallness* is not "thrust upon" the young, whose lives lie ahead of them. Much is at stake here.

CHAPTER 7

—————

GLOBALIZATION
AND VOICE

The world is both spectacularly rich and distressingly impoverished. There is unprecedented opulence in contemporary living, and the massive command over resources, knowledge, and technology that we now take for granted would have been hard for our ancestors to imagine. But ours is also a world of dreadful poverty and appalling deprivation. An astounding number of children are ill fed, ill clad, ill treated, and also illiterate and needlessly ill. Millions perish *every week* from diseases that could be completely eliminated, or at least prevented from killing with abandon. Depending on where they are born, children can have the means and facilities for great prosperity or face the likelihood of desperately deprived lives.

Massive inequalities in the opportunities different people have encourages skepticism about the ability of globalization to serve the interests of the underdogs. Indeed, a hardened sense of frustration is well reflected in the slogans of protest movements of so-called antiglobalization activists. Moved by the thesis that global relations are primarily antagonistic and adversarial, rather than mutually supportive, the protesters want to rescue the underdogs of the world from what they see as the penalties of globalization. Criticisms of globalism have not only been thunderously expressed in the demonstrations that continue to take place around the world, in Seattle, Washington, Quebec, Madrid, London, Melbourne, Genoa, Edinburgh, and elsewhere. These concerns also get sympathetic attention from a much larger number of people who may not want to join the vehement demonstrations, but to whom too the asymmetries of sharply distanced fortunes appear quite unfair and reprehensible. Some see in these inequalities a total failure also of any moral force a global identity may be expected to induce.

Voice, Veracity, and Public Reasoning

I will argue presently that it is a mistake to see the deprivations and divided lives as penalties of globalization, rather than as failures of social, political, and economic arrangements, which are entirely contingent and not inescapable companions of global closeness. Nevertheless, I would also argue that the so-called antiglobalization critiques can—and often do—make a positive and important contribution in helping to raise a number of serious questions for public discussion which have to be considered and appraised. A serious diagnosis of causes can be somewhat misplaced and yet help to initiate an enlightening inquiry into what needs to be done to overcome the serious problems that undoubtedly exist.

As Francis Bacon noted four hundred years ago (in 1605), in

his treatise *The Advancement of Learning*: "The registering and proposing of doubts have a *double* use." One use is straightforward: it guards us "against errors." The second use, Bacon argued, involved the role of doubts in initiating and furthering a process of inquiry, which can have the effect of enriching our understanding. Issues that "would have been passed by lightly without intervention," Bacon noted, end up being "attentively and carefully observed" precisely because of the "intervention of doubts."[1]

Raising serious questions about globalization and the nature of the global economy can make a constructive dialectical contribution even when there is room for much skepticism about the particular slogans that are used, especially by youthful and boisterous protesters. There may be fine reasons to be doubtful about the allegedly evil consequences of global economic relations, which make arresting headlines as summaries of the antiglobalization perspective. It is necessary to scrutinize closely the momentous issues that the protesters can—and often do—bring to the fore, and this is itself a contribution of considerable importance. Indeed, the debates that are thus initiated can serve as the basis of global public reasoning on significant issues. Since democracy is primarily about public reasoning (as was discussed in chapter 3), the debates generated by these "global doubts" can be seen as elementary but possibly important contributions toward practicing some form of (necessarily primitive) global democracy.[2]

Critique, Voice, and Global Solidarity

I will presently go into the substantive questions raised by the protesters, and by others skeptical of globalization, and I shall also have to examine the counterarguments presented by the defenders of globalization. But before that, I want to comment briefly on the nature of global identity involved—explicitly or by implication—in these debates. Some overarching critics of globalization see themselves as forcefully pointing to the deplorable absence, in a heartless world, of an effective sense of global solidarity. Certainly, there is much to be depressed about in the manifest lack of an effective global morality in dealing with deeply distressing international issues.

But do we really live in a morally sequestered world? If a sense of a global solidarity is really so nonsensical, why should so many people around the world (including the "antiglobalization" protesters and indeed a great many others) be so upset about the state of the world and argue passionately—if noisily—for a better deal for the disadvantaged and deprived? The protesters themselves come from all over the world—they are not just local inhabitants of Seattle or Melbourne or Genoa or Edinburgh. The dissidents try to work together to protest about what they see as serious iniquity or injustice that plagues the people of the world.

Why should women and men from one part of the world worry about the fact that people in other parts of the world are getting a raw deal if there is no sense of global belonging and no concern about global unfairness? Global discontent, to which the protest movements give voice (sometimes, admittedly, a very rough voice), can be seen as evidence of the existence of a sense of global identity and some concern about global ethics.

I must presently discuss why the term "antiglobalization" is not a good description of the nature of the discontent that goes under that name. But no matter what we call it, that borderless discontent is itself a major global phenomenon, both in terms of the subject of its concern (including its implicitly humanitarian ethics and inclusive politics) and in the form of the wide interest and involvement it generates across the world.

The sense of extensive identity underlying these concerns goes well beyond the borders of nationality, culture, community, or religion. It is hard to miss the powerfully inclusive idea of belonging that moves so many people to challenge what they see as unfairness that divides the world population. Indeed, the so-called antiglobalization critique is perhaps the most globalized moral movement in the world today.

Intellectual Solidarity

All of this adds to the importance of paying serious attention to the subject matter of the antiglobalization critique. Even though globalization is one of the most discussed topics in the contemporary world, it is not altogether a well-defined concept. A multitude of global interactions are put under the broad heading of globalization, varying from the expansion of cultural and scientific influences across borders to the enlargement of economic and business relations throughout the world. A wholesale rejection of globalization would not only go against global business, it would also cut out movements of ideas, understanding, and knowledge that can help all the people of the world, including the most disadvantaged members of the world population. A comprehensive rejection of globalization can thus be powerfully counterproductive. There is a strong need to separate out the different questions that appear merged together in the rhetoric of the antiglobalization protests. The globalization of knowledge deserves a particularly high-profile recognition, despite all the good things that can be rightly said about the importance of "local knowledge."

Globalization is often seen, both in journalistic discussions and in remarkably many academic writings, as a process of Westernization. Indeed, some who take an upbeat—indeed celebratory—view of the phenomenon even see it as a contribution of Western civilization to the world. In fact, there is a nicely stylized history that goes with this allegedly no-nonsense reading. It all happened in Europe: first came the Renaissance, then the Enlightenment and the Industrial Revolution, and this led to a massive rise in living standards in the West. And now those great achievements of the West are spreading to the world. Globalization, in this view, is not only good, it is also a gift of the West to the world. The champions of this reading of history tend to feel upset not only by the way this great benefaction is taken by many people to be a curse, but also by the way the West's highly beneficial bestowal to the world is spurned and castigated by an ungrateful non-Western world. Like many good stylized stories, this one too has a grain of truth in it, but there is much fantasy too, which, as it happens, feeds an artificial global divide.

There is another—in some respects an "opposite"—story, which also receives attention and plays a seriously diverting role. This accepts Western dominance as central to globalization, but attributes to it the nasty features associated with globalization. In these criticisms, the allegedly "Western" character of globalization is often given a prominent and damaging role (this is easily seen in the rhetoric of the ongoing protest movements). Indeed, globalization is sometimes seen as a correlate of Western dominance—indeed a continuation of Western imperialism. While different parts of the antiglobalization movements have different concerns and priorities, the resentment of Western dominance certainly plays a significant role in many of these protests. There is clearly an "anti-Western" element in parts of the antiglobalization movement. The celebration of non-Western identities of various types (discussed in chapters 4 through 6), related to religion (such as Islamic fundamentalism), or region (such as Asian values), or culture (such as Confucian ethics), can add fuel to the fire of global separatism.

To start off our critical inquiry, it can be asked: "Is globalization really a new Western curse?" I would argue that it is, in general, neither new, nor necessarily Western, nor a curse. Indeed, globalization has, over thousands of years, contributed to the progress of the world, through travel, trade, migration, the spread of cultural influences, and the dissemination of knowledge and understanding (including that of science and technology). These global interrelations have often been very productive in the advancement of different countries in the world. And the active agents of globalization have sometimes been located quite far from the West.

To illustrate, let me look back at the beginning of the last millennium rather than at its end. Around A.D. 1000, the global spread of science, technology, and mathematics was changing the nature of the old world, but the dissemination then was, to a great extent, in the opposite direction to what we see today. For example, the high technology in the world of A.D. 1000 included the clock and the iron-chain suspension bridge, the kite and the magnetic compass, paper and printing, the crossbow and gunpowder, the wheelbarrow and the rotary fan. Each one of these examples of high technology of the world a millennium ago was well established and extensively used in China, and was practically unknown elsewhere. Globalization spread them across the world, including Europe.

In his *Critical and Miscellaneous Essays,* Thomas Carlyle claims that "the three great elements of modern civilization" are "Gunpowder, Printing, and the Protestant Religion." While the Chinese cannot be praised—or blamed—for the origin of Protestantism, the Chinese contribution to Carlyle's list of civilizational ingredients covers two of the three items, namely gunpowder and printing. This is, however, less comprehensive than the Chinese bestowal, in the form of a clean sweep, in Francis Bacon's list of ingredients of civilization in *Novum Organum*, published in 1620, "printing, gunpowder, and the magnet."

A similar movement occurred, as was discussed in chapter 3, in the Eastern influence on Western mathematics. The decimal system emerged and became well developed in India between the second and sixth centuries, and was used extensively also by Arab mathematicians soon thereafter. Mathematical and scientific innovations in South and West Asia were pioneered by a galaxy of intellectuals, such as Aryabhata, Brahmagupta, and al-Khwarizmi. These works reached Europe mainly in the last quarter of the tenth century, and began having a major impact in the early years of the last millennium, playing a significant part in the scientific revolution that helped to transform Europe. Insofar as anything can be said about the identity of the agents of globalization, that identity is neither exclusively Western, nor regionally European, nor necessarily linked to Western dominance.

The Parochial versus the Global

The misdiagnosis that globalization of ideas and practices must be resisted because they entail "Westernization" has played quite a regressive part already in the colonial and postcolonial world (as was briefly discussed in chapter 5). It incites a regionally narrow outlook and also undermines the advancement of science and knowledge, cutting across borders. Indeed, it is not only counterproductive in itself, it can also end up being a good way for non-Western societies to shoot themselves in the foot—even in their precious cultural foot.

Let me illustrate the peculiarly reactionary nature of this "localist" outlook. Consider the resistance in India to the use of Western ideas and concepts in science and mathematics in the nineteenth century. This debate in British India fit into the broader controversy about focusing either on Western education or (as if this would be an exclusive alternative) on indigenous Indian education; this was seen as an unbridgeable dichotomy. The "Westernizers," such as the redoubtable T. B. Macaulay—the powerful British administrator who wrote, in 1835, the tremendously influential "Minute" on Indian education—saw no merit in Indian tradition whatever. As he explained, "I have never found one among them [advocates of Indian languages and tradition] who could deny that a single shelf of a good European library was worth the whole native literature of India and Arabia."[3] Partly in retaliation, the advocates of native education resisted Western imports altogether, preferring traditional scholarship and classical Indian education. But both sides seemed to accept that there must be, to a great extent, a necessary exclusiveness in each approach.

However, given the interrelation between cultures and civilizations, this presumption was bound to produce some very awkward classificatory problems. A sharp illustration of the nature of extensive international relations is provided by the arrival in India of the trigonometric term "sine" directly from Western trigonometry. That modern term (that is, "sine") came straight from the British in the mid-nineteenth century, which took the place of the old Sanskrit concepts, and this was seen as just another example of the Anglo-Saxon invasion of Indian culture.

And yet, amusingly enough, "sine" actually came from India itself, through various transformations, from a good Sanskrit name for that critically important trigonometric concept. Indeed, the migration of the concept and the terminology give some idea of the nature of the historical—and distinctly "premodern"—globalization of ideas. The fifth-century Indian mathematician Aryab-hata had developed and made extensive use of the concept of "sine": he called it *jya-ardha*, which literally means "chord-half" in Sanskrit. From there the term moved on in an interesting migra-tory way, as Howard Eves describes in his *History of Mathematics*:

> Aryabhata called it *ardha-jya* ("half-chord") and *jya-ardha* ("chord-half"), and then abbreviated the term by simply using *jya* ("chord"). From *jya* the Arabs phonetically derived *jiba,* which, following Arabic practice of omitting vowels, was written as *jb*. Now *jiba,* aside from its technical significance, is a meaningless word in Arabic. Later writers who came across *jb* as an abbrevi-ation for the meaningless word *jiba* substituted *jaib* instead, which contains the same letters, and is a good Arabic word meaning "cove" or "bay." Still later, Gherardo of Cremona (ca. 1150), when he made his translations from the Arabic, replaced the Arabian *jaib* by its Latin equivalent, *sinus* [meaning a cove or a bay], from whence came our present word *sine*.[4]

Given the cultural and intellectual interconnections in world history, the question of what is "Western" and what is not would be hard to decide. In fact, Aryabhata's *jya* was translated into Chi-nese as *ming* and was used in such widely used tables as *yue jian-liang ming,* literally "sine of lunar intervals." If Macaulay had understood the world's intellectual history somewhat better, he would have had to broaden his gaze from the "single shelf" of Euro-pean books which he admired so much. His Indianist opponents too would have to be less distrustful of the Western shelves.

Indeed, Europe would have been a lot poorer—economically, culturally, and scientifically—had it resisted the globalization of mathematics, science, and technology coming from China, India, Iran, and the Arab world, at the beginning of the second millennium. And the same applies, though in the reverse direction, today. To reject the globalization of science and technology on the ground that this is Western imperialism (as some protesters suggest) would not only amount to overlooking global contributions—drawn from many different parts of the world—that lie solidly behind so-called Western science and technology, but would also be quite a daft practical decision given the extent to which the whole world can benefit from the process of intellectual give-and-take. To equate this phenomenon with imperialism or with European colonialism of ideas and beliefs (as the rhetoric often suggests) would be a serious and costly error, in the same way that a European rejection of Eastern influence on science and mathematics would have been at the beginning of the last millennium.

We must not, of course, overlook the fact that there are issues related to globalization that actually do connect with imperialism. The history of conquests, colonial dominance, alien rule, and the humiliation of conquered people remains relevant today in many different ways (as was discussed earlier, particularly in chapter 5). But it would be a great mistake to see globalization primarily as a feature of imperialism. It is a much bigger—and immensely greater—process than that.

Economic Globalization and Inequality

Antiglobalization protesters belong, however, to several different camps, and some opponents of "economic globalization" have no problem whatever with the globalization of ideas (including that of science and literature). Their views, which need careful attention, are certainly not dismissable on the ground that the globalization of science, technology, and understanding has made very positive contributions to the world—something that these particular critics of economic globalization would not at all deny.

However, as it happens, many positive achievements specifically of economic globalization are also visible in different parts of the world. We can hardly fail to see that the global economy has brought much greater material prosperity to quite a few different areas on the globe, such as Japan, China, and South Korea, and to varying extents elsewhere as well, from Brazil to Botswana. Pervasive poverty dominated the world a few centuries ago, with only a few pockets of rare affluence. Lives were fairly uniformly "nasty, brutish and short," as Thomas Hobbes put it in his classic book *Leviathan,* published in 1651. In overcoming that penury, extensive economic interrelations between nations as well as economic incentives for the development and use of modern methods of production have been enormously influential and helpful.

It would be hard to believe that the progress of the living conditions of the poor across the world can be made faster by withholding from them the great advantages of contemporary technology, the valuable opportunity to trade and exchange, and the social as well as economic merits of living in open, rather than closed, societies. People from very deprived countries clamor for the fruits of modern technology (such as the use of newly invented medicines, particularly in the treatment of AIDS—these new drugs have transformed the lives of AIDS patients in America and Europe); they seek greater access to the markets in the richer countries for a wide variety of commodities, from sugar to textiles; and they want more voice and attention in the affairs of the world. If there is skepticism of the results of globalization, it is not because suffering humanity wants to withdraw into its shell.

In fact, the preeminent practical challenges today include the possibility of making good use of the remarkable benefits of economic connections, technological progress, and political opportunity in a way that pays adequate attention to the interests of the deprived and the underdog. This is not, in fact, a question of rubbishing global economic relations, but of making the immense benefits of globalization more fairly shared. Despite the terminology chosen by the "antiglobalization" movements, the central issue in the reproach has to relate, in one way or another, to the real existence and resilience of massive global inequality and poverty, rather than to the alleged fruitfulness of doing without global economic relations.

Global Poverty and Global Fairness

So what about global inequality and poverty? The distributional questions that figure—in an explicit or implicit form—in the rhetoric both of the so-called antiglobalization protesters and of the no-nonsense "proglobalization" defenders need some critical scrutiny. Indeed, this issue has suffered, I would argue, from the popularity of some oddly unfocused questions.

It is argued by some "antiglobalization" resisters that the central problem is that the rich in the world are getting richer, and the poor poorer. This is by no means uniformly so (even though there are a number of cases, particularly in Latin America and Africa, in which this has actually happened), but the crucial issue is whether this is the right way to understand the central issues of fairness and equity in the global economy today.

On the other side, the enthusiasts for no-nonsense globalization often invoke—and draw greatly on—their understanding that the poor in the world are typically getting less poor, not (as often alleged) more impoverished. They refer in particular to the evidence that those among the poor who participate in trade and exchange are not getting any poorer—quite the contrary. Since they are getting richer through being involved in the global economy, ergo (the argument runs) globalization is not unjust to the poor: "The poor benefit too—so what's the gripe?" If the centrality of this question were accepted, then the whole debate would turn on determining which side is right in this mainly empirical dispute: "Are the globally engaged poor getting poorer *or* richer (tell us, tell us, which it is)?"

But is this really the right question to ask? I would argue that it absolutely is *not*. There are two problems in this way of seeing the unfairness issue. The first is the need to recognize that given the global facilities that exist today, including problems of omission as well as commission (to be discussed presently), many people find it hard to enter the global economy at all. The concentration on those who are gainfully engaged in trade leaves out millions who remain excluded—and effectively unwelcome—from the activities of the privileged. Exclusion is as important a problem here as unequal inclusion. The remedying of such exclusion would demand radical departures in domestic economic policies (such as greater facilities for basic education, health care, and microcredit at home), but they also call for changed international policies of other, particularly richer, countries. For one thing, economically more advanced countries can make a big difference by being more welcoming to commodities—agricultural goods as well as textiles and other products of industries—exported from the developing world. There are issues also of humane—and realistic—treatment of past debts that limit the freedom of the poorer countries so much (it is most welcome that some initial steps have been taken in that direction in recent years).[5] There is also the big issue of aid and development assistance, on which political opinions differ, but which is by no means an irrelevant focus of attention.[6] There are many other issues to be tackled as well, including the need to rethink the ongoing legal provisions, such as the present system of patent rights (I shall return to these questions presently).

The second issue, however, is more complex and in greater need of a clearer understanding. Even if the poor who are engaged in the globalized economy were becoming just a little richer, this need not imply that the poor are getting a *fair* share of the benefits of economic interrelations and of its vast potential. Nor is it adequate to ask whether international inequality is getting marginally larger or smaller. To rebel against the appalling poverty and staggering inequalities that characterize the contemporary world, or to protest against unfair sharing of the benefits of global cooperation, it is not necessary to claim that the inequality not only is terribly large, but is also getting marginally *larger*.

The issue of fairness in a world of different groups and disparate identities demands a fuller understanding. When there are gains from cooperation, there can be many alternative arrangements that benefit each party compared with no cooperation. The division of benefits can widely vary despite the need for cooperation (this is sometimes called "cooperative conflict").[7] For example, there may be considerable gains from the setting up of new industries, but there still remains the problem of the division of benefits between workers, capitalists, sellers of inputs, buyers (and consumers) of outputs, and those benefiting indirectly from the increased income in the localities involved. The divisions involved would depend on relative prices, wages, and other economic parameters that would govern exchange and production. It is appropriate, therefore, to ask whether the distribution of gains is *fair or acceptable,* and not just whether there *exist* some gains for all parties in comparison with no cooperation (which can be the case for a great many alternative arrangements).

As John Nash, the mathematician and game theorist (and now also a household name thanks to the enormously successful film based on Sylvia Nasar's wonderful biography, *A Beautiful Mind*), discussed more than half a century ago (in a paper published in 1950, which was among his writings cited by the Royal Swedish Academy in awarding him the Nobel Prize in economics in 1994), the central issue is not whether a particular arrangement is better for all than no cooperation at all, which would be true of many alternative arrangements. Rather, the principal question is whether the particular divisions to emerge, among the various alternatives available, are fair divisions, given what could be chosen instead.[8] A criticism that a distributional arrangement that goes with cooperation is unfair (whether aired in the context of industrial relations or family arrangements or international institutions) cannot be rebutted by merely noting that all the parties are better off than would be the case in the absence of cooperation (well reflected in the supposedly telling argument: "The poor benefit too—so what's the gripe?"). Since this would be true of very many—possibly infinitely many—alternative arrangements, the real exercise does not lie there, but rather in the choice *among* these various alternatives with different distributions of gains for all of the parties.

The point can be illustrated with an analogy. To argue that a particularly unequal and sexist family arrangement is unfair, it does not have to be shown that women would have done comparatively better had there been no families at all ("If you think that the ongoing family divisions are unfair to women, why don't you go and live outside families?"). That is not the issue—women seeking a better deal within the family are not proposing, as an alternative, the possibility of living without families. The bone of contention is whether the sharing of the benefits within the family system is seriously unequal in the existing institutional arrangements, compared with what alternative arrangements can be made. The consideration on which many of the debates on globalization have concentrated, to wit, whether the poor too benefit from the established economic order, is an entirely inadequate focus for assessing what has to be assessed. What must be asked instead is whether they can feasibly get a better—and fairer— deal, with less disparities of economic, social, and political opportunities, and if so, through what international and domestic rearrangements this could be brought about. That is where the real engagement lies.

The Possibility of More Fairness

There are, however, some preliminary issues to be discussed first. Is a fairer global deal possible without upsetting the globalized system of economic and social relations altogether? We must ask, in particular, whether the deal that the different groups get from globalized economic and social relations can be changed without undermining or destroying the benefits of a global market economy? The conviction, which is often implicitly invoked in antiglobalization critiques, that the answer must be in the negative has played a critically important part in generating gloom and doom about the future of the world with global markets, and this is what gives the so-called antiglobalization protests their chosen name. There is, in particular, an oddly common presumption that there is such a thing as "*the* market outcome," no matter what rules of private operation, public initiatives, and nonmarket institutions are combined with the existence of markets. That answer is, in fact, entirely mistaken, as is readily ascertained.

Use of the market economy is consistent with many different

ownership patterns, resource availabilities, social facilities, and rules of operation (such as patent laws, antitrust regulations, provisions for health care and income support, etc.). And depending on these conditions, the market economy itself would generate distinct sets of prices, terms of trades, income distributions, and, more generally, very different overall outcomes.[9] For example, every time public hospitals, schools, or colleges are set up, or resources transferred from one group to another, the prices and quantities reflected in the market outcome inescapably alter. Markets do not—and cannot—act alone. There is no "*the* market outcome" irrespective of the conditions that govern the markets, including the distribution of economic resources and ownerships. Introduction or enhancement of institutional arrangements for social security and other supportive public interventions can also yield significant differences in the outcome.

The central question is not—indeed cannot be—whether or not to use the market economy. That shallow question is easy to answer. No economy in world history has ever achieved widespread prosperity, going beyond the high life of the elite, without making considerable use of markets and production conditions that depend on markets. It is not hard to conclude that it is impossible to achieve general economic prosperity without making extensive use of the opportunities of exchange and specialization that market relations offer. This does not deny at all the basic fact that the operation of the market economy can certainly be significantly defective under many circumstances, because of the need to deal with goods that are collectively consumed (such as public health facilities) and also (as has been much discussed recently) because of the importance of asymmetric—and more generally imperfect—information that different participants in the market economy may have.[10] For example, the buyer of a used car knows far less about the car than the owner selling it does, so that people have to make their exchange decisions in partial ignorance and in particular with unequal knowledge. These problems, which are significant and serious, can, however, be addressed through appropriate public policies that supplement the working of the market economy. But it would be hard to dispense with the institution of markets altogether without thoroughly undermining the prospects of economic progress.

Indeed, using markets is not entirely unlike speaking prose. It is not easy to dispense with it, but much depends on what prose we choose to speak. The market economy does not work alone in *globalized* relations—indeed it cannot operate alone even *within* a given country. It is not only the case that a market-inclusive over-all system can generate widely different results depending on various enabling conditions (such as how physical resources are distributed, how human resources are developed, what rules of business relations prevail, what social insurances are in place, how extensively technical knowledge is shared, and so on), but also these enabling conditions themselves depend critically on economic, social, and political institutions that operate nationally and globally.

As has been amply demonstrated in empirical studies, the nature of market outcomes are massively influenced by public policies in education and literacy, epidemiology, land reform, microcredit facilities, appropriate legal protection, etc., and in each of these fields there are things to be done through public action that can radically alter the outcome of local and global economic relations. It is this class of interdependences that have to be understood and utilized to alter the inequalities and asymmetries that characterize the world economy. Mere globalization of market relations can, on its own, be a deeply inadequate approach to world prosperity.

Omissions and Commissions

There are many difficult problems to be faced in working for fairer economic and social arrangements in the world. There is, for example, considerable evidence that global capitalism is typically much more concerned with markets than with, say, establishing democracy, or expanding public education, or enhancing social opportunities of the underdogs of society. Multinational firms can also exert substantial influence on the priorities of public expenditure in many third-world countries in the direction of giving preference to the convenience of the managerial classes and privileged workers over the removal of widespread illiteracy, medical deprivation, and other handicaps of the poor.[11] These adverse connections, observable in Latin America, Africa, and also parts of Asia, have to be faced and tackled. While they may not impose an insurmountable barrier to equitable development, it is important that the surmountable barriers be clearly diagnosed and actually surmounted.

The continued inequities in the global economy are closely related to various institutional failures that have to be overcome. In addition to the momentous *omissions* that need to be rectified, there are also serious problems of *commission* that must be addressed for elementary global justice. Many of these problems have been discussed extensively in the literature.[12] However, some of these issues demand greater attention in public discussion than has happened so far.

An oddly underdiscussed global "commission" that causes intense misery as well as lasting deprivation concerns, as was discussed in the last chapter, the involvement of the world powers in the globalized trade in arms (nearly 85 percent of the arms sold internationally in recent years were sold by the G8 countries, the great powers that have a major role in leading the world).[13] This is a field in which a new global initiative is urgently required, going beyond the need—the very important need—to curb terrorism, on which the focus is so heavily concentrated right now.

Injurious commissions also include severely restrictive—and inefficient—trade barriers that curb exports from the poorer countries. Another important issue is that of inequitable patent laws which can serve as counterproductive hurdles for the use of lifesaving drugs—needed for diseases like AIDS—which can often be produced very cheaply, but the market price of which are pushed high up by the burden of royalties. While it is certainly important not to create economic conditions such that the innovative research of pharmaceuticals dries out, there are, in fact, plenty of intelligent compromise arrangements, including facilities for variable pricing, that can provide good incentives for research while allowing the poor of the world to buy these vitally important drugs. It must be remembered that the nonbuying of drugs by the poor which they cannot afford to buy can hardly add anything to the incentives of the drug producers; the issue is to combine efficiency-based considerations with demands of equity, in an intelligent and humane way, with an adequate understanding of the demands of global efficiency as well as justice.

The counterproductive patent regimes that exist—and rule—at the moment also provide very inadequate incentive for medical research aimed at developing new medicines (including nonrepeating vaccines) that would be particularly useful for the poorer people of the world whose ability to offer a high price for such medicines is quite limited. The reach of incentives in producing medical innovations of specific benefit to low-income people can be puny indeed. This is well reflected in the heavy bias of pharmaceutical research in the direction of catering to those with more income to spend. Given the nature of the market economy and the role that the profit calculations inescapably play in its operation, the concentration has to be on departures that can change the incentive pattern radically. They can vary from altered legal arrangements for intellectual property rights (including differing tax treatment of profits from different types of innovations) to providing public incentives through specially devised programs of support.[14] The demands of economic globalization are not confined only to joining the market economy and freeing trade and exchange (important though they often are), but extend also to making the institutional arrangements more fair and equitable for the distribution of gains from economic intercourse.[15]

Enhancement of domestic arrangements can also be crucial to the way globalization affects people who are brought more into global exchange. For example, while forces of competition may drive some traditional producers out of their customary jobs, the displaced people cannot easily find new jobs by entering into new enterprises linked to the global economy if they happen to be illiterate and unable to read instructions and follow the new demands of quality control, or if they are burdened by illnesses that impair their productivity and mobility.[16] With such handicaps, they can get the sticks of the global economy without tasting the carrots. The remedying of these barriers requires the development of facilities for schooling and education, and also of a supportive safety network, including health care. Economic globalization is not just about opening up the markets.

Indeed, the global market economy is as good as the company it keeps.[17] Global voices—from far and near—can help globalization, including global markets, to have better companions. There is a world to be won on behalf of humanity, and global voices can help us to achieve this.

Poverty, Violence, and the Sense of Injustice

If religion and community are associated with global violence in the minds of many people, then so are global poverty and inequality. There has, in fact, been an increasing tendency in recent years to justify policies of poverty removal on the ground that this is the surest way to prevent political strife and turmoil. Basing public policy—international as well as domestic—on such an understanding has some evident attractions. Given the public anxiety about wars and disorder in the rich countries in the world, the indirect justification of poverty removal—not for its own sake but for the sake of peace and quiet in the world—provides an argument that appeals to self-interest for helping the needy. It presents an argument for allocating more resources on poverty removal because of its presumed political, rather than moral, relevance.

While the temptation to go in that direction is easy to understand, it is a perilous route to take even for a worthy cause. Part of the difficulty lies in the possibility that if wrong, economic reductionism would not only impair our understanding of the world, but would also tend to undermine the declared rationale of the public commitment to remove poverty. This is a particularly serious concern, since poverty and massive inequality are terrible enough in themselves, and deserve priority even if there were no connection whatever with violence. Just as virtue is its own reward, poverty is at least its own penalty. This is not to deny that poverty and inequality can—and do—have far-reaching connections with conflict and strife, but these connections have to be examined and investigated with appropriate care and empirical scrutiny, rather than being casually invoked with unreasoned rapidity in support of a "good cause."

Destitution can, of course, produce provocation for defying

established laws and rules. But it need not give people the initiative, courage, and actual ability to do anything very violent. Destitution can be accompanied not only by economic debility, but also by political helplessness. A starving wretch can be too frail and too dejected to fight and battle, and even to protest and holler. It is thus not surprising that often enough intense and widespread suffering and misery have been accompanied by unusual peace and silence.

Indeed, many famines have occurred without there being much political rebellion or civil strife or intergroup warfare. For example, the famine years in the 1840s in Ireland were among the most peaceful, and there was little attempt by the hungry masses to intervene even as ship after ship sailed down the river Shannon laden with rich food, carrying it from starving Ireland to well-fed England, which had greater purchasing power. The Irish do not have a great reputation for pliant docility, and yet the famine years were, by and large, years of law and order (with very few exceptions). Looking elsewhere, my own childhood memories in Calcutta during the Bengal famine of 1943 include the sight of starving people dying in front of sweetshops with various layers of luscious food displayed behind glass windows, without a single glass being broken, or law and order being disrupted. The Bengalis have been responsible for many violent rebellions (one against the Raj occurred even in 1942, in the year preceding the famine of 1943), but things were quiet in the famine year itself.

The issue of timing is particularly important, since a sense of injustice can feed discontent over a very long period, much after the debilitating and disabling effects of a famine and deprivation are over. The memory of destitution and devastation tends to linger, and can be invoked and utilized to generate rebellion and violence. The Irish famines of the 1840s may have been peaceful times, but the memory of injustice and the social bitterness about political and economic neglect had the effect of severely alienating the Irish from Britain, and contributed greatly to the violence that characterized Anglo-Irish relations over more than 150 years. Economic destitution may not lead to any immediate violence, but it would be wrong to presume from this that there is no connection between poverty, on the one hand, and violence on the other.

The neglect of the plight of Africa today can have a similarly long-run effect on world peace in the future. What the rest of the world (especially the richer countries) did—or did not do—when at least a quarter of the African population seemed to be threatened with extinction through epidemics, involving AIDS, malaria, and other maladies, might not be forgotten for a very long time to come. We have to understand more clearly how poverty, deprivation, and neglect, and the humiliations associated with asymmetry of power, relate over long periods to a proneness to violence, linked with confrontations that draw on grievances against the top dogs in a world of divided identities.

Neglect can be reason enough for resentment, but a sense of encroachment, degradation, and humiliation can be even easier to mobilize for rebellion and revolt. Israel's ability to displace, repress, and rule over Palestinians, assisted by military power, has extensive and long-run consequences that go well beyond whatever immediate political gains they may be currently bringing to Israel. The sense of injustice in the arbitrary violation of the rights of Palestinians remains in readiness to be recruited for what, from the opposite end, is seen as violent "retaliation." The vengeance might come not only from Palestinians, but also from much larger groups of people linked with Palestinians through Arab, Muslim, or third-world identities. The sense that the world is divided between haves and have-nots greatly helps in the cultivation of discontent, opening up the possibilities of recruitment in the cause of what is often seen as "retaliatory violence."

In order to understand how this works, it is necessary to distinguish between the leaders of violent insurrection and the much larger populations on whose support the leaders rely. Leaders like Osama bin Laden do not—to say the least—suffer from poverty and have no economic reason whatever for feeling left out from sharing the fruits of global capitalism. And yet the movements that are led by well-off leaders typically do rely greatly on a sense of injustice, iniquity, and humiliation that the established world order is seen as having produced. Poverty and economic inequality may not instantly breed terrorism or influence the leaders of terrorist organizations, but nevertheless they can help to create rich recruiting grounds for the foot soldiers of the terrorist camps.

Second, tolerance of terrorism by an otherwise peaceful population is another peculiar phenomenon in many parts of the contemporary world, particularly where there is a sense of having been badly treated, for example, because of being left behind by global economic and social progress, or where there is a strong memory of having been politically roughed up in the past. A more equitable sharing of the benefits of globalization can contribute to long-run preventive measures both (1) against the recruitment of the cannon fodder of terrorism, and (2) against the creation of a general climate where terrorism is tolerated (and sometimes even celebrated).

Even though poverty and a sense of global injustice may not lead immediately to an eruption of violence, there are certainly connections there, operating over a long period of time, that can have a significant effect on the possibility of violence. The memory of ill treatment of the Middle East by Western powers many decades—perhaps even a hundred years—ago, which still linger in various forms in West Asia, can be cultivated and magnified by the commanders of confrontation to enhance the ability of terrorists to recruit volunteers for violence. The anger with the Soviet Union particularly linked with its Afghan policy may have been seen by American strategists as a nicely usable weapon in the cold war, but it was open to redirection against the Western world through the solitarist view of an Islamic identity confronting Europe and America (the distinction between a capitalist US and a Communist USSR would not matter much in that singular perspective). In that twofold classification, the rhetoric of global injustice is torn away from its constructive correlates, and is deployed instead, in a suitably adapted form, to feed an atmosphere of violence and retribution.

Awareness and Identity

Indeed, alternative ways of responding to inequalities and the sense of global injustice can, to some extent, compete with each other for the attention of people of the world today. The very diagnosis that, in one perspective, motivates a search for global equity can also, in another light, be good material to be twisted, narrowed, and harshened to feed the cause of global vengeance.

Much would depend on how the issue of identity is addressed in assessing the implications of global inequality. It can take us in several different directions. The one that is being used with devastating effect is the cultivation and exploitation of discontent caused by perceptions of past humiliations or present disparities, building on some solitarist contrast of identity, particularly through a "West–anti-West" formulation (discussed in chapter 5). We are seeing a lot of this right now, supplementing and—to some extent—feeding a bellicose religious (particularly Islamic) identity ready to confront the West. This is a world of singularly divided identities where the economic and political contrasts are made to fit—as a "subtheme"—into differences in religious ethnicity.

Happily, that is not the only way in which global inequalities, and past and present humiliations, can be addressed. First, a constructive response can come from addressing global inequalities and grievances more explicitly, with a fuller understanding of the real issues involved and possible directions of remedy (with which much of this chapter has been concerned). Second, a constructive role can also be played by globalization itself, not only through the prosperity that can be generated—and more equitably shared—by the operation of global economic relations supplemented by other institutional arrangements (discussed earlier), but also through the beyond-border concerns that can result from extensive human contacts generated by global economic closeness.

The world has shrunk a great deal in recent times through closer integration, quicker communication, and easier access. However, already two and a quarter centuries ago, David Hume spoke about the contribution of increased economic and social relations in expanding the reach of our sense of identity and the coverage of our concern about justice. In *An Enquiry Concerning the Principles of Morals,* published in 1777, Hume pointed to these connections (in a chapter called "Of Justice"):

> [A]gain suppose that several distinct societies maintain a kind of intercourse for mutual convenience and advantage, the boundaries of justice still grow larger, in proportion to the largeness of men's views, and the force of their mutual connexions. History, experience, reason sufficiently instruct us in this natural progress of human sentiments, and in the gradual enlargement of our regards to justice, in proportion as we become acquainted with the extensive utility of that virtue.[18]

Hume was speaking about the possibility that trade and economic connections between countries can enhance distant people's involvement with each other. As people come in closer touch with each other, they can begin to take an interest in faraway persons whose existence may have been only dimly perceived earlier.

Widespread interest in global inequalities and asymmmetries, of which antiglobalization protests are a part, can be seen as something of an embodiment of what David Hume was talking about in his claim that closer economic relations would bring distant people within the reach of "the gradual enlargement of our regards to justice." This fits in with the claim, presented earlier, that the voices of global protest are part of the newly developing ethics of globalization in the contemporary world. Even though the critique of equity-neglecting global capitalism often stops at mere denunciation, it can easily be extended to demand more global equity through appropriate institutional modifications.

"Antiglobalization" critiques, which focus on the unequal and unjust deals that the underdogs of the world get, cannot be sensibly seen (given the strong use of global ethics in these critiques) as being really antiglobalization. The motivating ideas suggest the need for seeking a fairer deal for the deprived and the miserable, and for a more just distribution of opportunities in a suitably modified global order. Global discussion of the urgency of these issues can be the basis of a constructive search for the ways and means of reducing global injustice. That search is critically important in itself, and that must be the first—and main—thing to say about it. But it can also have a very substantial role in taking us away from the confrontation of sharply divisive identities. It makes a difference how we choose to see ourselves.

CHAPTER 8

MULTICULTURALISM AND FREEDOM

Demand for multiculturalism is strong in the contemporary world. It is much invoked in the making of social, cultural, and political policies particularly in Western Europe and America. This is not at all surprising, since increased global contacts and interactions, and in particular extensive migrations, have placed diverse practices of different cultures next to each other. The general acceptance of the exhortation to "love thy neighbor" might have emerged when the neighbors led, by and large, much the same kind of life ("let's continue this conversation next Sunday morning when the organist takes a break"), but the same entreaty to love one's neighbors now requires people to take an interest in the very diverse living modes of proximate people. The globalized nature of the contemporary world does not allow the luxury of ignoring the difficult questions multiculturalism raises.

The subject of this book—ideas of identities and their relation to violence in the world—is closely linked with the understanding of the nature, implications, and merits (or demerits) of multiculturalism. There are, I would argue, two basically distinct approaches to multiculturalism, one of which concentrates on the promotion of diversity as a value in itself; the other approach focuses on the freedom of reasoning and decision-making, and celebrates cultural diversity to the extent that it is as freely chosen as possible by the persons involved. These themes have briefly been discussed earlier in this book (particularly in chapter 6), and they fit also into a broad approach to social progress in general—"development as freedom"—I have tried to defend elsewhere.[1] But the issues demand a closer examination in the particular context of assessing the practice of multiculturalism today, particularly in Europe and America.

One of the central issues must be how human beings are seen. Should they be categorized in terms of inherited traditions, particularly the inherited religion, of the community in which they happen to be born, taking that unchosen identity to have automatic priority over other affiliations involving politics, profession, class, gender, language, literature, social involvements, and many other connections? Or should they be understood as persons with many affiliations and associations the priorities over which they must themselves choose (taking the responsibility that comes from reasoned choice)? Also, should we assess the fairness of multiculturalism primarily by the extent to which people from different cultural backgrounds are "left alone," or by the extent to which their ability to make reasoned choices is positively supported through social opportunities of education and participation in civil society and the political and economic processes ongoing in the country? There is no way of escaping these rather foundational questions if multiculturalism is to be fairly assessed.

In discussing the theory and practice of multiculturalism, it is useful to pay particular attention to the British experience. Britain has been in the forefront of promoting inclusive multiculturalism, with a mixture of successes and difficulties, which are of relevance also to other countries in Europe and the United States.[2] Britain did have race riots in London and Liverpool in 1981 (though not quite as momentous as in France in the fall of 2005), and these led to further efforts toward integration. Things have been fairly stable and calm over the last quarter of a century. The process of integration in Britain has been greatly helped by the fact that all British residents from the Commonwealth countries, from where most nonwhite immigrants have come to Britain, have full voting rights in Britain immediately, even without British citizenship. Integration has also been helped by largely nondiscriminatory treatment of immigrants in health care, schooling, and social security. Despite all this, however, Britain has recently experienced the alienation of a group of immigrants, and also fully homegrown terrorism when some young Muslims from immigrant families— born, educated, and reared in Britain—killed a great many people in London through suicide bombings.

Discussions of British policies on multiculturalism thus have a much wider reach, and arouse much greater interest and passion, than the boundaries of the ostensible subject matter would lead one to expect. Six weeks after the terrorist attacks in London in the summer of 2005, when Le Monde, the leading French newspaper, presented a critique under the title "The British Multicultural Model in Crisis," the debate was immediately joined by a leader of another liberal establishment, James A. Goldston, director of the Open Society Justice Initiative in America, who described the Le Monde article as "trumpeting," and replied:

"Don't use the very real threat of terrorism to justify shelving more than a quarter century of British achievement in the field of race relations."[3] There is a general issue of some importance to be debated and evaluated here.

I will argue that the real issue is not whether "multiculturalism has gone too far" (as Goldston summarizes one of the lines of criticism), but what particular form multiculturalism should take. Is multiculturalism nothing other than the tolerance of diversity of cultures? Does it make a difference who chooses the cultural practices, whether they are imposed in the name of "the culture of the community" or whether they are freely chosen by persons with adequate opportunity to learn and reason about alternatives? What facilities do members of different communities have, in schools as well as in the society at large, to learn about the faiths—and non-faiths—of different people in the world and to understand how to reason about choices that human beings must, if only implicitly, make?

Britain's Achievements

Britain, where I first came as a student in 1953, has been particularly impressive in making room for different cultures. The distance traveled has been, in many ways, quite extraordinary. I recollect (with some fondness, I must admit) how worried my first landlady in Cambridge was about the possibility that my skin color might come off in the bath (I had to assure her that my hue was agreeably sturdy and durable), and also the care with which she explained to me that writing was a special invention of Western civilization ("the Bible did it"). For someone who has lived— intermittently but for long periods—through the powerful evolution of British cultural diversity, the contrast between Britain today and Britain half a century ago is just amazing.

The encouragement given to cultural diversity has certainly made many contributions to the lives of people. It has helped Britain to become an exceptionally lively place in many different ways. From the joys of multicultural food, literature, music, dancing, and the arts to the befuddling entrapment of the Notting Hill Carnival, Britain gives its people—of all the different backgrounds—much to relish and celebrate. Also, the acceptance of cultural diversity (as well as voting rights and largely nondiscriminatory public services and social security, referred to earlier) has made it easier for people with very different origins to feel at home.

It is, however, worth recalling that the acceptance of diverse living modes and of varying cultural priorities has not always had an easy ride even in Britain. There has been a periodic but persistent demand that immigrants give up their traditional lifestyles and adopt the dominant living modes in the society to which they have immigrated. That demand has sometimes taken a remarkably detailed view of culture, involving quite minute behavioral issues, well illustrated by the famous "cricket test" proposed by the redoubtable Lord Tebbit, the justly famous Conservative political leader. The test indicates that a well-integrated immigrant cheers for England in test matches against the country of the person's origin (such as Pakistan) when the two sides play each other.

To say something positive first, Tebbit's "cricket test" has the enviable merit of definiteness, and gives an immigrant a marvelously clear-cut procedure for establishing his or her integration into British society: "Cheer for the English cricket team and you will be fine!" The immigrant's job in making sure that he or she is really integrated into British society could otherwise be quite exacting, if only because it is no longer easy to identify what the dominant lifestyle in Britain actually is, to which the immigrant must conform. For example, curry is now so omnipresent in the British diet that it features as "authentic British fare" according to the British Tourist Board. In the 2005 General Certificate of Secondary Education (GCSE) examinations taken by schoolchildren when they are around sixteen, two of the questions included in the "Leisure and Tourism" paper were: "Other than Indian food, name one other type of food often provided by take-away restaurants," and "Describe what customers need to do to receive a delivery service from an Indian take-away restaurant." Reporting on the 2005 GCSE, the conservative *Daily Telegraph* complained, not about any cultural bias in these nationwide exams, but about the "easy" nature of the questions, which anyone in Britain should be able to answer without any special training.[4]

I also recollect seeing, not long ago, a definitive description of the unquestionable Englishness of an Englishwoman in a London paper: "She is as English as daffodils or chicken tikka masala." Given all this, a South Asian immigrant to Britain might be a bit confused, but for Tebbit's kindly help, about what will count as a surefire test of being distinctively British to which the outside entrant has to conform. The important issue underlying what may be seen as the frivolity of the foregoing discussion is that cultural contacts are currently leading to such a hybridization of behavioral modes across the world that it is difficult to identify any "local culture" as being genuinely indigenous, with a timeless quality.[5] But thanks to Lord Tebbit, the task of establishing Britishness can become nicely algorithmic and wonderfully easy (indeed as easy as answering the GCSE questions just cited).

Lord Tebbit has gone on to suggest, recently, that had his "cricket test" been put to use, it would have helped to prevent the terrorist attacks by British-born militants of Pakistani origin: "[H]ad my comments been acted on, those attacks would have been less likely."[6] It is difficult to avoid the thought that this confident prediction perhaps underestimates the ease with which any would-be terrorist—with or without training from Al Qaeda—could pass the "cricket test" of cheering for the English cricket team without changing his behavior pattern one iota in any other way.

I don't know how much into cricket Lord Tebbit himself is. If you enjoy the game, cheering for one side or the other is determined by a number of varying factors, including, of course, one's national loyalty or residential identity, but also the quality of play and the overall interest of a match—and a series. Wanting a particular outcome often has a contingent quality which would make it hard to insist on unvarying and unfailed rooting for any team (England or any other). Despite my Indian origin and nationality, I must confess that I have sometimes cheered for the Pakistani cricket team, not only against England, but also against India. During the Pakistani team's tour of India in 2005, when Pakistan lost the first two one-day matches in the series of six, I cheered for Pakistan for the third match, to keep the series alive and interesting. In the event, Pakistan went well beyond my hopes and won all of the remaining four matches to defeat India soundly by the margin of four to two (another instance of Pakistan's "extremism" of which Indians complain so much!).

A more serious problem lies in the obvious fact that admonitions of the kind enshrined in Tebbit's cricket test are entirely irrelevant to the duties of British citizenship or residence, such as participation in British politics, joining British social life, or desisting from making bombs. They are also quite distant from anything that may be needed to lead a fully cohesive life in the country.

These points were quickly seized in postimperial Britain, and despite the diversions of such invitations as Tebbit's cricket test, the inclusionary nature of British political and social traditions made sure that varying cultural modes within the country could be seen as being entirely acceptable in a multiethnic Britain. There are, not surprisingly, many natives who continue to feel that this historical trend is a great mistake, and that disapproval is often combined with severe resentment that Britain has become such a multiethnic country at all (in my last encounter with a resenter, at a bus stop, I was suddenly told, "I have seen through you all," but I was disappointed that my informant declined to tell me more about what he had found). But the weight of British public opinion is, or at least has been until recently, quite strongly in the direction of tolerating—and even celebrating—cultural diversity.

All this and the inclusionary role of voting rights and nondiscriminatory public services (discussed earlier) have contributed to interracial calm of a kind that France in particular has not enjoyed recently. It does, however, still leave some of the central issues of multiculturalism entirely unresolved, and I want to take them up now.

Problems of Plural Monoculturalism

One important issue concerns the distinction between multiculturalism and what may be called "plural monoculturalism." Does the existence of a diversity of cultures, which might pass each other like ships in the night, count as a successful case of multiculturalism? Since Britain is currently torn between *interaction* and *isolation,* the distinction is centrally important (and has a bearing even on terrorism and violence).

To comment on the distinction involved, let me begin with a contrast by noting that Indian and British food can genuinely claim to be multicultural. India had no chili until the Portuguese brought it to India from America, but it is effectively used in a wide range of Indian food today and seems to be a dominant element in most types of curries. It is, for example, plentifully present in a mouth-burning form in vindaloo, which, as the name indicates, carries the immigrant memory of combining wine with potatoes. Also, tandoori cooking might have been perfected in India, but it originally came to India from West Asia. Curry powder, on the other hand, is a distinctly English invention, unknown in India before Lord Clive, and evolved, I imagine, in the British army mess. And we are beginning to see the emergence of new styles of preparing Indian food, offered in sophisticated subcontinental restaurants in London.

In contrast, having two styles or traditions coexisting side by side, without the twain meeting, must really be seen as "plural monoculturalism." The vocal defense of multiculturalism that we frequently hear these days is very often nothing more than a plea for plural monoculturalism. If a young girl in a conservative immigrant family wants to go out on a date with an English boy, that would certainly be a multicultural initiative. In contrast, the attempt by her guardians to stop her from doing this (a common enough occurrence) is hardly a multicultural move, since it seeks to keep the cultures sequestered. And yet it is the parents' prohibition, which contributes to plural monoculturalism, that seems to get most of the vocal and loud defense from alleged multiculturalists, on the ground of the importance of honoring traditional cultures, as if the cultural freedom of the young woman were of no relevance whatever, and as if the distinct cultures must somehow remain in secluded boxes.

Being born in a particular social background is not in itself an exercise of cultural liberty (as was discussed earlier), since it is not an act of choice. In contrast, the decision to stay firmly *within* the traditional mode would be an exercise of freedom if the choice is made after considering other alternatives. In the same way, a decision to *move away*—by a little or a lot—from the received behavior pattern, arrived at after reflection and reasoning, would also qualify as such an exercise. Indeed, cultural freedom can frequently clash with cultural conservatism, and if multiculturalism is defended in the name of cultural freedom, then it can hardly be seen as demanding unwavering and unqualified support for staying steadfastly within one's inherited cultural tradition.

The second question relates to the fact, much discussed in this book, that while religion or ethnicity may be an important identity for people (especially if they have the freedom to choose between celebrating or rejecting inherited or attributed traditions), there are other affiliations and associations people also have reason to value. Unless it is defined very oddly, multiculturalism cannot override the right of a person to participate in civil society, or to take part in national politics, or to lead a socially nonconformist life. And furthermore, no matter how important multiculturalism is, it cannot lead automatically to giving priority to the dictates of traditional culture over all else.

As was discussed earlier, the people of the world cannot be seen merely in terms of their religious affiliations—as a federation of religions. For much the same reasons, a multiethnic Britain can hardly be seen as a collection of ethnic communities. However, the "federational" view has gained much support in contemporary Britain. Indeed, despite the tyrannical implications of putting persons into rigid boxes of given "communities," that view is frequently interpreted, rather bafflingly, as an ally of individual freedom. There is even a much-aired "vision" of "the future of multi-ethnic Britain" that sees it as "a looser federation of cultures held together by common bonds of interest and affection and a collective sense of being."[7]

But must a person's relation to Britain be *mediated through* the "culture" of the family in which he or she has been born? A person may decide to seek closeness with more than one of these predefined cultures or, just as plausibly, with none. Also, a person may well decide that her ethnic or cultural identity is less important to her than, say, her political convictions, or her professional commitments, or her literary persuasions. It is a choice for her to make, no matter what her place is in the strangely imagined "federation of cultures."

These are not abstract concerns, nor are they specific features of the complexity of modern life. Consider the case of an early arrival of a South Asian to the British Isles. Cornelia Sorabji came to Britain from India in the 1880s, and her identities reflected the varieties of affiliations she, like others, had. She was variously described by herself and others as an "Indian" (she did eventually return to India and wrote an engaging book called *India Calling*), as being at home in England as well ("homed in two countries, England and India"), as a Parsee ("I am Parsee by nationality"), as a Christian (full of admiration for "the early martyrs of the Christian Church"), as a sari-clad woman ("always perfectly dressed in a richly coloured silk sari," as the *Manchester Guardian* described her), as a lawyer and barrister-at-law (at Lincoln's Inn), as a fighter for women's education and for legal rights particularly for secluded women (she specialized as a legal adviser to veiled women, "purdahnaschins"), as a committed supporter of the British Raj (who even accused Mahatma Gandhi, not particularly fairly, for enrolling "babies as early as six and seven years of age"), always nostalgic about India ("the green paroquets at Budh Gaya: the blue wood-smoke in an Indian village"), as a firm believer in the asymmetry between women and men (she was proud to be seen as "a modern woman"), as a teacher at an exclusively men's college ("at eighteen, in a Male College"), and as "the first woman" ever of *any* background to get the degree of bachelor of civil law at Oxford (requiring "a special decree from Congregation to allow her to sit").[8] Cornelia Sorabji's choices must have been influenced by her social origin and background, but she made her own decisions and chose her own priorities.

There would be serious problems with the moral and social claims of multiculturalism if it were taken to insist that a person's identity must be defined by his or her community or religion, over-looking all the other affiliations a person has (varying from language, class, and social relations to political views and civil roles), and through giving automatic priority to inherited religion or tradition over reflection and choice. And yet that narrow approach to multiculturalism has assumed a preeminent role in some of the official British policies in recent years.

The state policy of actively promoting new "faith schools," freshly devised for Muslim, Hindu, and Sikh children (in addition to preexisting Christian ones), which illustrates this approach, is not only educationally problematic, it encourages a fragmentary perception of the demands of living in a desegregated Britain. Many of these new institutions are coming up precisely at a time when religious prioritization has been a major source of violence in the world (adding to the history of such violence in Britain itself, including Catholic-Protestant divisions in Northern Ireland—not unconnected themselves with segmented schooling). Prime Minister Blair is certainly right to note that "there is a very strong sense of ethos and values in those schools."[9] But education is not just about getting children, even very young ones, immersed in an old, inherited ethos. It is also about helping children to develop the ability to reason about new decisions any grown-up person will have to take. The important goal is not some formulaic "parity" in relation to old Brits with their old faith schools but what would best enhance the capability of the children to live "examined lives" as they grow up in an integrated country.

The Priority of Reason

The central issue was put a long time ago with great clarity by Akbar, the Indian emperor, in his observations on reason and faith in the 1590s. Akbar, the Great Mughal, was born a Muslim and died a Muslim, but he insisted that faith cannot have priority over reason, since one must justify—and if necessary reject—one's inherited faith through reason. Attacked by traditionalists who argued in favor of instinctive faith, Akbar told his friend and trusted lieutenant Abul Fazl (a formidable scholar in Sanskrit as well as Arabic and Persian, with much expertise in different religions, including Hinduism as well as Islam):

> The pursuit of reason and rejection of traditionalism are so brilliantly patent as to be above the need of argument. If traditionalism were proper, the prophets would merely have followed their own elders (and not come with new messages).[10]

Reason had to be supreme, since even in disputing reason, we would have to give reasons.

Convinced that he had to take a serious interest in the diverse religions of multicultural India, Akbar arranged for recurring dialogues involving (as was discussed earlier) not only people from mainstream Hindu and Muslim backgrounds in sixteenth-century India, but also Christians, Jews, Parsees, Jains, and even the followers of "Carvaka"—a school of atheistic thinking that had robustly flourished in India for more than two thousand years from around the sixth century B.C.[11]

Rather than taking an "all or nothing" view of a faith, Akbar liked to reason about particular components of each multifaceted religion. For example, arguing with Jains, Akbar would remain skeptical of their rituals, and yet became convinced by their argument for vegetarianism and even ended up deploring the eating of all flesh in general. Despite the irritation all this caused among those who preferred to base religious belief on faith rather than reasoning, he stuck to what he called "the path of reason" (*rahi aql*), and insisted on the need for open dialogue and free choice. Akbar also claimed that his own Islamic religious beliefs came from reasoning and choice, not from "blind faith," nor from what he called "the marshy land of tradition."

There is also the further question (particularly relevant to Britain) about how the *non*immigrant communities should see the demands of multicultural education. Should it take the form of leaving each community to conduct its own special historical celebrations, without responding to the need for the "old Brits" to be more fully aware of the global interrelations in the origins and development of world civilization (discussed in chapters 3 through 7)? If the roots of so-called Western science or culture draw inter alia on, say, Chinese innovations, Indian and Arabic mathematics, or West Asian preservation of the Greco-Roman heritage (with, for example, Arabic translations of forgotten Greek classics being retranslated into Latin many centuries later), should there not be a fuller reflection of that robust interactive past than can be found, at this time, in the school curriculum of multiethnic Britain? The priorities of multiculturalism can differ a great deal from those of a plural monocultural society.

If one issue concerning faith schools involves the problematic nature of giving priority to unreasoned faith over reasoning, there is another momentous issue here, which concerns the role of religion in categorizing people, rather than using other bases of classification. People's priorities and actions are influenced by all of their affiliations and associations, not merely by religion. For example, the separation of Bangladesh from Pakistan, as was discussed earlier, was based on reasons of language and literature, along with political priorities, not on religion, which both wings of undivided Pakistan shared. To ignore everything other than faith is to obliterate the reality of concerns that have moved people to assert their identities that go well beyond religion.

The Bangladeshi community, large as it is in Britain, is merged in the religious accounting into one large mass along with all the other coreligionists, with no further acknowledgment of culture and priorities. While this may please the Islamic priests and religious leaders, it certainly shortchanges the abundant culture of that country and emaciates the richly diverse identities that Bangladeshis have. It also chooses to ignore altogether the history of the formation of Bangladesh itself. There is, as it happens, an ongoing political struggle at this time *within* Bangladesh between secularists and their detractors (including religious fundamentalists), and it is not obvious why British official policy has to be more in tune with the latter than with the former.

The political importance of the issue can hardly be exaggerated. The problem, it must be admitted, did not originate with recent British governments. Indeed, official British policy has for many years given the impression that it is inclined to see British citizens and residents originating from the subcontinent primarily in terms of their respective communities, and now—after the recent accentuation of religiosity (including fundamentalism) in the world—community is defined primarily in terms of faith, rather than taking account of more broadly defined cultures. The problem is not confined to schooling, nor of course to Muslims. The tendency to take Hindu or Sikh religious leaders as spokesmen for the British Hindu or Sikh population, respectively, is also a part of the same process. Instead of encouraging British citizens of diverse backgrounds to interact with each other in civil society, and to participate in British politics as citizens, the invitation is to act "through" their "own community."

The limited horizons of this reductionist thinking directly affects the living modes of the different communities, with particularly severe constraining effects on the lives of immigrants and their families. But going beyond that, as the events of 2005 in Britain show, how citizens and residents see themselves can also affect the lives of others. For one thing, the vulnerability to influences of sectarian extremism is much greater if one is reared and schooled in the sectarian (but not necessarily violent) mode. The British government is seeking to stop the preaching of hatred by religious leaders, which must be right, but the problem is surely far more extensive than that. It concerns whether citizens of immigrant backgrounds should see themselves as members of particular communities and specific religious ethnicities first, and only *through* that membership see themselves as British, in a supposed federation of communities. It is not hard to understand that this uniquely fractional view of any nation would make it more open to the preaching and cultivation of sectarian violence.

Tony Blair has good reason to want to "go out" and have debates about terror and peace "inside the Muslim community" and to "get right into the entrails of [that] community."[12] Blair's dedication to fairness and justice is hard to dispute. And yet the future of multiethnic Britain must lie in recognizing, supporting, and helping to advance the many different ways in which citizens with distinct politics, linguistic heritage, and social priorities (along with different ethnicities and religions) can interact with each other in their different capacities, including *as citizens*. Civil society in particular has a very important role to play in the lives of all citizens. The participation of British immigrants—Muslims as well as others—should not be primarily placed, as it increasingly is, in the basket of "community relations," and seen as being mediated by religious leaders (including "moderate" priests and "mild" imams, and other agreeable spokesmen of religious communities).

There is a real need to rethink the understanding of multiculturalism both to avoid conceptual disarray about social identity and also to resist the purposeful exploitation of the divisiveness that this conceptual disarray allows and even, to some extent, encourages. What has to be particularly avoided (if the foregoing analysis is right) is the confusion between multiculturalism with cultural liberty, on the one side, and plural monoculturalism with faith-based separatism on the other. A nation can hardly be seen as a collection of sequestered segments, with citizens being assigned fixed places in predetermined segments. Nor can Britain be seen, explicitly or by implication, as an imagined national federation of religious ethnicities.

Gandhi's Arguments

There is an uncanny similarity between the problems Britain faces today and those that British India faced, and which Mahatma Gandhi thought were getting direct encouragement from the Raj. Gandhi was critical in particular of the official view that India was a collection of religious communities. When Gandhi came to London for the "Indian Round Table Conference" called by the British government in 1931, he found that he was assigned to a specific sectarian corner in the revealingly named "Federal Structure Committee." Gandhi resented the fact that he was being depicted primarily as a spokesman for Hindus, in particular "caste Hindus," with the remaining half of the Indian population being represented by delegates, chosen by the British prime minister, of each of the "other communities."

Gandhi insisted that while he himself was a Hindu, the political movement he led was staunchly universalist and not a community-based movement; it had supporters from all of the different religious groups in India. While he saw that a distinction can be made along religious lines, he pointed to the fact that other ways of dividing the population of India were no less relevant. Gandhi made a powerful plea for the British rulers to see the *plurality* of the diverse identities of Indians. In fact, he said he wanted to speak not for Hindus in particular, but for "the dumb, toiling, semi-starved millions" who constitute "over 85 per cent of the population of India."[13] He added that, with some extra effort, he could speak even for the rest, "the Princes . . . the landed gentry, the educated class."

Gender was another basis for an important distinction which, Gandhi pointed out, the British categories ignored, thereby giving no special place to considering the problems of Indian women. He told the British prime minister, "[Y]ou have had, on behalf of the women, a complete repudiation of special representation," and went on to point out that "they happen to be one half of the population of India." Sarojini Naidu, who came with Gandhi to the Round Table Conference, was the only woman delegate in the conference. Gandhi mentioned the fact that she was elected as the president of the Congress Party, overwhelmingly the largest political party in India (this was in 1925, which was, as it happens, fifty years before any woman was elected to preside over any major British political party, to wit, Margaret Thatcher in 1975). Sarojini Naidu could, on the Raj's "representational" line of reasoning, speak for half the Indian people, namely Indian women; Abdul Qaiyum, another delegate, pointed also to the fact that Sarojini Naidu, whom he called "the Nightingale of India," was also the one distinguished poet in the assembled gathering, a different kind of identity from being seen as a Hindu politician.

In a meeting arranged at the Royal Institute of International Affairs during that visit, Gandhi also insisted that he was trying to resist "the vivisection of a whole nation."[14] Gandhi was not, of course, ultimately successful in his attempt at "staying together," though it is known that he was in favor of taking more time to negotiate—to prevent the partition of 1947—than the rest of the Congress leadership found acceptable. Gandhi would have been extremely pained also by the violence against Muslims that was organized by sectarian Hindu leaders in his own state of Gujarat in 2002.[15] He would, however, have been relieved by the massive condemnation these barbarities received from the Indian population at large, which influenced the heavy defeat, in the Indian general elections that followed (in May 2004), of the parties implicated in the violence in Gujarat.

Gandhi would have taken some comfort in the fact, not unrelated to his point in the 1931 Round Table Conference in London, that India, with more than 80 percent Hindu population, is led today by a Sikh prime minister (Manmohan Singh) and headed by a Muslim president (Abdul Kalam), with its ruling party (Congress) being presided over by a woman from a Christian background (Sonia Gandhi). Such mixtures of communities can be seen in most walks of Indian life, from literature and cinema to business and sports, and they are not seen as anything particularly special. It is not just that Muslims occupy the position of being, for example, the richest businessman (indeed the wealthiest person) in India (Azim Premji), or having captained the Indian cricket team (Pataudi and Azharuddin), or the first serious international star in women's tennis (Sania Mirza), but also that all of them are seen, in these contexts, as Indians in general, not as Indian Muslims in particular.

During the recent parliamentary debate on the judicial report on the killings of Sikhs that occurred immediately after Indira

Gandhi's assassination by her Sikh bodyguard, the Indian prime minister, Manmohan Singh, told the Indian parliament, "I have no hesitation in apologising not only to the Sikh community but to the whole Indian nation because what took place in 1984 is the negation of the concept of nationhood and what is enshrined in our Constitution."[16] Manmohan Singh's multiple identities are very much in prominence here when he apologized, in his role as prime minister of India and a leader of the Congress Party (which was also in office in 1984), to the Sikh community, of which he is a member (with his omnipresent blue turban), and to the whole Indian nation, of which he is, of course, a citizen. All this might be very puzzling if people were to be seen in the "solitarist" perspective of only one identity each, but the multiplicity of identities and roles fits very well with the fundamental point Gandhi was making at the London conference.

Much has been written about the fact that India, with more Muslim people than almost every Muslim-majority country in the world (and with nearly as many Muslims, more than 145 million, as Pakistan), has produced extremely few homegrown terrorists acting in the name of Islam, and almost none linked with Al Qaeda. There are many causal influences here (including, as the columnist and author Thomas Friedman has argued, the influence of the growing and integrated Indian economy).[17] But some credit must also go to the nature of Indian democratic politics, and to the wide acceptance in India of the idea, championed by Mahatma Gandhi, that there are many identities other than religious ethnicity that are also relevant for a person's self-understanding and for the relations between citizens of diverse backgrounds within the country.

I recognize that there is something a little embarrassing for me, as an Indian, to claim that, thanks to the leadership of Mahatma Gandhi and others (including the clearheaded analysis of "the idea of India" by the greatest Indian poet, Rabindranath Tagore, who described his family background as "a confluence of three cultures, Hindu, Mohammedan and British"), India has been able, to a considerable extent, to avoid indigenous terrorism linked to Islam, which currently threatens a number of Western countries, including Britain. But Gandhi was expressing a very general concern, not specific to India, when he asked, "Imagine the whole nation vivisected and torn to pieces; how could it be made into a nation?"

That query was motivated by Gandhi's deep worries about the future of India. The problem, however, is not specific to India and can arise for other nations too, including the country that ruled India until 1947. The disastrous consequences of defining people by their religious ethnicity and giving predetermined priority to the community-based perspective over all other identities, which Gandhi thought was receiving support from India's British rulers, may well have come, alas, to haunt the country of the rulers themselves.

In the Round Table Conference in 1931, Gandhi did not get his way, and even his dissenting opinions were only briefly recorded, with no mention of where the dissent came from. In a gentle complaint addressed to the British prime minister, Gandhi said at the meeting, "[I]n most of these reports you will find that there is a dissenting opinion, and in most of the cases that dissent unfortunately happens to belong to me." Gandhi's farsighted refusal to see a nation as a federation of religions and communities did not, however, "belong" only to him. It belongs also to a world that is willing to see the serious problem to which Gandhi was drawing attention. It can belong today to Britain too. At least I hope so.

CHAPTER 9

FREEDOM
TO THINK

M y first exposure to murder occurred when I was eleven. This was in 1944, in the communal riots that characterized the last years of the British Raj, which ended in 1947. I saw a profusely bleeding unknown person suddenly stumbling through the gate to our garden, asking for help and a little water. I shouted for my parents, while fetching some water for him. My father rushed him to the hospital, but he died there of his injuries. His name was Kader Mia.

The Hindu-Muslim riots that preceded independence also led the way to the partition of the country into India and Pakistan. The carnage erupted with dramatic suddenness, and it did not spare normally peaceful Bengal. Kader Mia was killed in Dhaka, then the second city—after Calcutta—of undivided Bengal, which would become, after the partition, the capital of East Pakistan. My

father taught at Dhaka University, and we lived in an area called
Wari in old Dhaka, not far from the university, in what happened
to be a largely Hindu area. Kader Mia was a Muslim, and no other
identity was relevant for the vicious Hindu thugs who had
pounced on him. In that day of rioting, hundreds of Muslims and
Hindus were killed by each other, and this would continue to happen day after day.

The sudden carnage seemed to come from nowhere, but it was
of course carefully orchestrated by sectarian prompting, linked in
different ways to the fervent political demands for the partition of
the country. The murderous riots would not last long; they would
soon evaporate from both sides of postpartition Bengal. The vehe-
mence of Hindu-Muslim violence would rapidly dissipate, giving
way to other views of oneself and others, bringing into prominence
other features of human identity. Indeed, my city of Dhaka would,
within a few years, burst into Bengali patriotism, with an intense
celebration of Bengali language, literature, music, and culture—
common to both the Muslims and the Hindus of Bengal. The
resurgence of an intense pride in the richness of a shared Bengali
culture had importance on its own, since it had been eclipsed so
severely during the bewildering fury of Hindu-Muslim violence.
But it had strong political correlates as well, linked particularly
with the resentment in East Pakistan (that is, the Bengali half of
Pakistan) of the severe inequality of political power, linguistic status, and economic opportunities between the two halves of the
imperfectly integrated Islamic state.

The alienation of Bengalis within Pakistan would eventually
lead, by December 1971, to the partition of Pakistan, and the formation of the new state of secular and democratic Bangladesh, with
Dhaka as its new capital. In the carnage that occurred in Dhaka in
March 1971, during the painful process of separation, with the Pak-

istani army's frenzied attempt to suppress the Bengali rebellion, the identity divisions were along the lines of language and politics, not religion, with Muslim soldiers from West Pakistan brutalizing—and killing—mainly Muslim dissenters (or suspected dissenters) in East Pakistan. From then the newly formed "Mukti Bahini" ("freedom brigade") fought for outright independence of Bangladesh from Pakistan. The identity division that fed the "struggle for liberation" was firmly linked to language and culture (and, of course, to politics), rather than to any religious difference.

Over sixty years after Kader Mia's death, as I try to recollect the deadly Hindu-Muslim riots in the 1940s, it is hard to convince myself that those terrible things did actually happen. But even though the communal riots in Bengal were entirely transitory and ephemeral (and the few cases in which riots have been fostered later on in other parts of India do not compare in size and reach with the events of the 1940s), they left in their wake thousands upon thousands of dead Hindus and Muslims. The political instigators who urged the killing (on behalf of what they respectively called "our people") managed to persuade many otherwise peaceable people of both communities to turn into dedicated thugs. They were made to think of themselves only as Hindus or only as Muslims (who must unleash vengeance on "the other community") and as absolutely nothing else: not Indians, not subcontinentals, not Asians, not members of a shared human race.

Even though the vast majority of both communities did not think in those narrowly frenzied terms, too many were suddenly trapped into that vicious mode of thinking, and the more savage among them—often at the troubled ends of each community— were induced to kill "the enemies who kill us" (as they were respectively defined). Many-sided persons were seen, through the hazy lenses of sectarian singularity, as having exactly one identity each, linked with religion or, more exactly, religious ethnicity (since being a nonpractitioner of one's inherited religion would not give a person any immunity whatever from being attacked).

Kader Mia, a Muslim day laborer, was knifed when he was on his way to a neighboring house, for work at a tiny wage. He was knifed on the street by some people who did not even know him and most likely had never set eyes on him before. For an eleven-year-old child, the event, aside from being a veritable nightmare, was profoundly perplexing. Why should someone suddenly be killed? And why by people who did not even know the victim, who could not have done any harm to the killers? That Kader Mia would be seen as having only one identity—that of being a member of the "enemy" community who "should" be assaulted and if possible killed—seemed altogether incredible. For a bewildered child, the violence of identity was extraordinarily hard to grasp. It is not particularly easy even for a still bewildered elderly adult.

While he was being rushed to the hospital in our car, Kader Mia told my father that his wife had asked him not to go into a hostile area during the communal riot. But he had to go out in search of work, for a little income, because his family had nothing to eat. The penalty of that necessity, caused by economic deprivation, turned out to be death. The terrible connection between economic poverty and comprehensive unfreedom (even the lack of freedom to live) was a profoundly shocking realization that hit my young mind with overpowering force.

Kader Mia died as a victimized Muslim, but he also died as a poor, unemployed laborer looking desperately for a bit of work and a small amount of money for his family to survive in very difficult times. The poorest members of any community are the easiest to kill in these riots, since they have to go out utterly unprotected in search of daily subsistence and their rickety shelters can easily be penetrated and ravaged by gangs. In the Hindu-Muslim riots, Hindu thugs killed poor Muslim underdogs with ease, while

Muslim thugs assassinated impoverished Hindu victims with abandon. Even though the community identities of the two groups of brutalized prey were quite different, their class identities (as poor laborers with little economic means) were much the same. But no identity other than religious ethnicity was allowed to count in those days of polarized vision focused on a singular categorization. The illusion of a uniquely confrontational reality had thoroughly reduced human beings and eclipsed the protagonists' freedom to think.

The Cultivation of Violence

Sectarian violence across the world is no less crude, nor less reductionist, today than it was sixty years ago. Underlying the coarse brutality, there is also a big conceptual confusion about people's identities, which turns multidimensional human beings into one-dimensional creatures. A person being recruited to join the Hutu killing mob in 1994 was being asked, if only implicitly, not to see himself as a Rwandan, or as an African, or as a human being (identities the targeted Tutsis shared), but only as a Hutu who was duty bound to "give the Tutsis their due." A Pakistani friend of mine, Shaharyar Khan, a highly respected senior diplomat who was sent by the secretary-general of the United Nations to Rwanda following the slaughter, told me later, "You and I have seen the beastliness of the riots in the subcontinent in the 1940s, but nothing had prepared me for the colossal magnitude of the killing that had occurred in Rwanda and for the comprehensiveness of the organized genocide there."[1] The butchery in Rwanda, and the related violence between Hutus and Tutsis in neighboring Burundi, took many more than a million lives within a span of a very few days.

Hating people is not easy. Ogden Nash's poem ("A Plea for Less Malice Toward None") got this just right:

> Any kiddie in school can love like a fool,
> But hating, my boy, is an art.

If we nevertheless see a great deal of hatred and violent conflict between different groups of people, the question that immediately arises is: "How does this 'art' work?"

The illusion of singular identity, which serves the violent purpose of those orchestrating such confrontations, is skillfully cultivated and fomented by the commanders of persecution and carnage. It is not remarkable that generating the illusion of unique identity, exploitable for the purpose of confrontation, would appeal to those who are in the business of fomenting violence, and there is no mystery in the fact that such reductionism is sought. But there is a big question about why the cultivation of singularity is so successful, given the extraordinary naïveté of that thesis in a world of obviously plural affiliations. To see a person exclusively in terms of only one of his or her many identities is, of course, a deeply crude intellectual move (as I have tried to argue in earlier chapters), and yet, judging from its effectiveness, the cultivated delusion of singularity is evidently easy enough to champion and promote. The advocacy of a unique identity for a violent purpose takes the form of separating out one identity group—directly linked to the violent purpose at hand—for special focus, and it proceeds from there to eclipse the relevance of other associations and affiliations through selective emphasis and incitement ("How could you possibly talk about these other things when our people are being killed and our women raped?").

The martial art of fostering violence draws on some basic instincts and uses them to crowd out the freedom to think and the possibility of composed reasoning. But it also draws, we have to recognize, on a kind of logic—a *fragmentary* logic. The specific identity that is separated out for special action is, in most cases, a genuine identity of the person to be recruited: a Hutu *is* indeed a Hutu, a "Tamil tiger" is clearly a Tamil, a Serb is not an Albanian, and a gentile German with a mind poisoned by Nazi philosophy is certainly a gentile German. What is done to turn that sense of self-understanding into a murderous instrument is (1) to ignore the relevance of all other affiliations and associations, and (2) to redefine the demands of the "sole" identity in a particularly belligerent form. This is where the nastiness as well as the conceptual confusions are made to creep in.

The Low Edge of High Theory

Even though asking people to confine their thoughts to only one identity each may seem to be a peculiarly crude invitation, it is worth recollecting that forcing people into boxes of singular identity is a feature also of many of the high theories of cultures and civilizations that are, in fact, quite influential right now (as I have also discussed in earlier chapters). These theories do not, of course, advocate or condone violence—indeed far from it. However, they try to understand human beings not as persons with diverse identities but predominantly as members of one particular social group—or community. Group memberships can, of course, be important (no serious theory of persons or individuals can ignore those social relationships), but the diminution of human beings involved in taking note only of one membership category for each person (neglecting all others) expunges at one stroke the far-reaching relevance of our manifold affinities and involvements.

For example, civilizational classifiers have often pigeonholed India as a "Hindu civilization"—a description that, among other things, pays little attention (as was discussed earlier) to India's more than 145 million Muslims (not to mention Indian Sikhs, Jains, Christians, Parsees, and others), and also ignores the extensive interconnections among the people of the country that do not work through religion at all, but through involvements in political, social, economic, commercial, artistic, musical, or other cultural activities. In a less straightforward way, the powerful school of communitarian thinking also hallows exactly *one identity per human being,* based on community membership, and in effect downplays all other affiliations that make human beings the complex and intricate social creatures that we are.

It is, in this context, interesting to recollect that communitarian thinking began, at least partly, as a constructive approach to identity, by trying to appreciate a person in his or her "social context."[2] But what began as an entirely estimable theoretical attempt at seeing human beings more "fully"—and more "socially"—has largely ended up with a highly restricted understanding of a person mainly as a member of exactly one group. That, alas, is not enough of a "social context," since each person has many different associations and attachments, the respective importance of which varies widely depending on the context. Despite the immensity of the vision implicit in the laudable task of "situating a person in the society" (which has repeatedly been invoked in social theories), the translation of that vision into actual application has often taken the form of neglecting the relevance of the person's plural social relations, seriously underestimating the richness of the multiple features of her "social situation." The underlying vision sees humanity in a drastically reduced form.

Penalties of Solitarist Illusion

The solitarist belittling of human identity has far-reaching conse-quences. An illusion that can be invoked for the purpose of divid-ing people into uniquely hardened categories can be exploited in support of fomenting intergroup strife. High theories with soli-tarist features like civilizational partitioning or communitarian confinement are not, of course, aimed in any way at sowing con-frontation—in fact quite the contrary. When, for example, a the-ory of "the clash of civilizations" is presented and promoted, the objective is to identify what is perceived as a preexisting reality (I have argued that this is done in a mistaken way, but that is a dif-ferent issue from motivation and impetus), and the theorists see themselves as "discovering" a confrontation, not creating—or adding to—one.

And yet theories can influence social thought, political action, and public policies. The artificial diminution of human beings into singular identities can have divisive effects, making the world potentially much more incendiary. For example, the reductionist characterization of India as a "Hindu civilization," referred to ear-lier, has drawn much applause from sectarian activists of the so-called Hindutva movement. Indeed, any conceptual categorization that could be seen as supporting their miniaturized view of India tends, naturally, to be invoked by that activist movement. The extremist wing of that movement even played a critically impor-tant part in the fostered violence in Gujarat in 2002, in which most of the victims, ultimately, were Muslims. Theories are sometimes taken more seriously in practical encounters than the theorists themselves anticipate. And when these theories are not only conceptually muddled but also readily usable for accentuating sectarian exclusion, they can be warmly welcomed by the leaders of social confrontation and violence.

Similarly, theories of Islamic exclusiveness, combined with ignoring the relevance of all the other identities Muslims have (in addition to their religious affiliations), can be utilized to provide the conceptual basis for a violent version of jihad (a pliable term that can be invoked for fierce incitement as well as for peaceful endeavor). The use of this route to fostered violence can be seen plentifully in the recent history of what is misleadingly called Islamic terrorism. The historical richness of different identities of Muslims, for example, as scholars, scientists, mathematicians, philosophers, historians, architects, painters, musicians, or writers, which have contributed so much to the past achievements of Muslim people (and to the global heritage of the world, discussed in chapters 3 through 6), can be overwhelmed—with a little help from theory—by the single-minded advocacy of a belligerently religious identity, with devastating effects.

As was discussed earlier, there is no reason why the discontented Muslim activists today have to concentrate only on the religious achievements of Islam, and not also on the great accomplishments of Muslims in many different fields, in deciding what they can do to change the contemporary world, which they associate with systematic humiliation and inequality. And yet the reductionism provided by a solitarist understanding of people, in terms exclusively of a belligerently religious identity, can be disastrously deployed by promoters of violent jihad to close all the other avenues Muslims can easily take, in line with their extensive historical traditions.

Similarly, on the other side, in resisting and fighting terrorism of this kind, there is good reason to invoke the richness of the many identities of human beings, not just their religious identity (on the exploitation of which terrorist recruitment of this kind relies). But, as was discussed earlier, the intellectual component of the resistance has tended to remain confined either to denouncing the religions involved (the bashing of Islam has been much used in this context) or to trying to define (or redefine) the religions to place them on the "right" side of the divide (invoking, for example, to use Tony Blair's appealing words, "the moderate and true voice of Islam"). While Islamic militants have good reason to deny all the identities of Muslims other than that of Islamic faith, it is not at all clear why those who want to resist that militancy also have to rely so much on the interpretation and exegesis of Islam, rather than drawing on the many other identities that Muslims also have.

Sometimes the singularity is even narrower than what the general category of being Islamic would allow. The distinction between Shias and Sunnis, for example, has been powerfully utilized for the purpose of sectarian violence between these two Muslim groups. From Pakistan to Iraq, that conflict adds another dimension to the violence of identity, defined in even more constricted terms. Indeed, as I finish writing this book, it is still unclear how much support the new Iraqi constitution will get from Sunni leaders, along with leaders of Shias and Kurds, and what could possibly happen in the future.

The integrity of Iraq is, of course, hampered by many historical factors, including the arbitrariness of its boundaries determined by Western colonialists and the inescapable divisiveness caused by an arbitrary and ill-informed military intervention. But, in addition, the sect-based political approach of the occupation leaders (not altogether different from the British official approach to colonial India about which Gandhi complained so much) has added much fuel to a preexisting fire.

The view of Iraq as a sum total of communities, with individuals being seen simply as Shia or Sunni or Kurd, has tended to dominate the Western reporting of Iraqi news, but it also reflects the way the politics of post-Saddam Iraq has developed. Sa' Doon al-Zubaydi (a member of the Iraqi constitutional committee) may tell James Naughtie of the BBC, "May I ask you to describe me as an Iraqi, not as a Sunni?"[3] But the combination of sectarian politics in Iraq and a muddled militarist undertaking of what is going on there makes it difficult to expect that the communal problems that Iraq and Baghdad face today can give way to anything broader and more national in that thoroughly troubled country.

Since the U.S.-led political initiative has tended to see Iraq as a collectivity of religious communities, rather than one of citizens, the negotiations have almost all been focused on the decisions and utterances of leaders of religious communities. This was certainly the easy way to proceed, given the tensions that already existed in the country and of course the new ones the occupation itself had created. But the easiest route in the short run is not always the best way to build the future of a country, especially when there is something extraordinarily important at stake, in particular the need for a nation to be a conglomeration of citizens, rather than a collectivity of religious ethnicities.

The problem was discussed earlier, particularly in the last chapter, in the context of a very different country, viz. Britain, which has an altogether dissimilar history and background. And yet the basic difficulty in seeing a country as a federation of communities, to which individuals belong *before* they belong to the nation, is present in both cases. Gandhi referred to the fostering and prioritization of such community-based unique identification as the "vivisection" of a nation, and there are good reasons for political concern about such sectionalization. It is also critically important to take note of the plurality of Iraqi identities, including gender and class as well as religion. One recollects Gandhi's reminder to the British prime minister, running the Raj in 1931, that women "happen to be one half of the population of India"— a line of thinking of some relevance to contemporary Iraq as well. The need to take note of these broader concerns in Iraq remains as strong today as they ever were.

The Role of Global Voices

The solitarist illusion has implications also for the way global identities are seen and invoked. If a person can have only one identity, then the choice between the national and the global becomes an "all or nothing" contest. And so does the contest between any global sense of belonging we may have and the local loyalties that may also move us. But to see the problem in these stark and exclusive terms reflects a profound misunderstanding of the nature of human identity, in particular its inescapable plurality. Recognizing the need to consider the claims of a global identity does not eliminate the possibility of paying much attention also to local and national problems. The role of reasoning and choice in the determination of priorities need not take that either-or form.

I have tried to identify earlier a number of economic, social, and political problems that have global dimensions, and the policy issues that relate to them, which have to be urgently addressed. There is, in particular, a strong case for institutional reforms that would facilitate the kind of change that would be needed to make globalization a fairer arrangement. The adversities faced by the vulnerable and the insecure have to be addressed on different fronts. The range of necessary actions varies from national policies (for example, the urgency of expanding the reach of education and public health care) to international initiatives and institutional reforms (related, for example, to global arrangements for curbing the arms trade, expanding the access of poorer countries to the markets of the richer economies, making patent laws and incentive systems more friendly to the development and usability of medicine needed by the poor of the world, and so on). These changes would be of importance on their own, but, as was discussed in chapter 7, they can also contribute to greater human security and restrain easy recruitment for terrorism and training. They can contribute, furthermore, to changing the climate of tolerance of violence, which is itself a factor in allowing terrorism to be nurtured in societies with deep grievances.

There is also an issue of intellectual fairness in dealing with global history, which is important both for a fuller understanding of the past of humanity (no mean task, that) and for overcoming the false sense of comprehensive superiority of the West that contributes to identity confrontation in an entirely gratuitous way. For example, while there has been some discussion recently—and rightly so—about the need for people of immigrant backgrounds in Europe or America to learn more about Western civilization, there is still extraordinarily little recognition of the importance that should be attached to the need for the "old Brits," "old Germans," "old Americans," and others to learn about the intellectual history of the world.

Not only were there remarkable achievements in different fields, from science, mathematics, and engineering to philosophy and literature, in the history of different parts of the world, but the foundations of many of the features of what are now called "Western civilization" and "Western science" were deeply influenced by contributions coming from different countries across the globe (as was discussed in chapters 3 through 7). Cultural or civilizational theories that ignore the role of "other" societies not only restrict the intellectual horizons of "old Europeans" or "old Americans," leaving their education peculiarly fragmentary, but also give the anti-Western movements a spurious sense of separation and conflict that helps to divide people along a largely artificial line of "West–anti-West" confrontation.

A Possible World

The point is often made, with evident justice, that it is impossible to have, in the foreseeable future, a democratic global state. This is indeed so, and yet if democracy is seen (as I have argued earlier that it should be) in terms of public reasoning, particularly the need for worldwide discussion on global problems, we need not put the possibility of global democracy in indefinite cold storage. It is not an "all or nothing" choice, and there is a strong case for advancing widespread public discussion, even when there would remain many inescapable limitations and weaknesses in the reach of the process. Many institutions can be invoked in this exercise of global identity, including of course the United Nations, but there is also the possibility of committed work, which has already begun, by citizens' organizations, many nongovernment institutions, and independent parts of the news media.

There is also an important role for the initiatives taken by a great many concerned individuals who are moved to demand that more attention be paid to global justice (in line with David Hume's expectation, cited earlier, that "the boundaries of justice still grow larger"). Washington and London may be irritated by the widely dispersed criticism of the coalition strategy in Iraq, just as Chicago or Paris or Tokyo may be appalled by the spectacular vilification of global business in parts of the so-called antiglobalization protests. The points that the protesters make are not invariably correct, but many of them do ask, as I have tried to illustrate, very relevant questions and thus contribute constructively to public reasoning. This is part of the way global democracy is already being initiated, without waiting for some gigantic global state to emerge in a fully institutionalized form.

There is a compelling need in the contemporary world to ask questions not only about the economics and politics of globalization, but also about the values, ethics, and sense of belonging that shape our conception of the global world. In a nonsolitarist understanding of human identity, involvement with such issues need not demand that our national allegiances and local loyalties be altogether *replaced* by a global sense of belonging, to be reflected in the working of a colossal "world state." In fact, global identity can begin to receive its due without eliminating our other loyalties.

In a very different context, dealing with his integrated understanding of the Caribbean (despite its immense varieties of races, cultures, preoccupations, and historical backgrounds), Derek Walcott wrote:

> I have never found that moment
> when the mind was halved by a horizon—
> for the goldsmith from Benares,
> the stonecutter from Canton,
> as a fishline sinks, the horizon
> sinks in the memory.[4]

In resisting the miniaturization of human beings, with which this book has been concerned, we can also open up the possibility of a world that can overcome the memory of its troubled past and subdue the insecurities of its difficult present. As an eleven-year-old boy I could not do much for Kader Mia as he lay bleeding with his head on my lap. But I imagine another universe, not beyond our reach, in which he and I can jointly affirm our many common identities (even as the warring singularists howl at the gate). We have to make sure, above all, that our mind is not halved by a horizon.

NOTES

CHAPTER 1.

The Violence of Illusion

1. Langston Hughes, *The Big Sea: An Autobiography* (New York: Thunder's Mouth Press, 1940, 1986), pp. 3–10.

2. See Robert D. Putnam, *Bowling Alone: The Collapse and the Revival of the American Community* (New York: Simon & Schuster, 2000).

3. There is considerable empirical evidence that ethnocentrism need not necessarily go with xenophobia (see, for example, Elizabeth Cashdan, "Ethnocentrism and Xenophobia: A Cross-cultural Study," *Current Anthropology* 42 (2001). And yet in many prominent cases ethnic, religious, racial, or other selective loyalties have been used in an exaggerated form to lead to violence against other groups. Vulnerability to "solitarist" instigation is the central issue here.

4. Jean-Paul Sartre, *Portrait of the Anti-Semite*, trans. Erik de Mauny (London: Secker & Warburg, 1968), p. 57.

5. *The Merchant of Venice*, act III, scene i, line 63.

6. See Alan Ryan, *J. S. Mill* (London: Routledge, 1974), p. 125. Mill noted that his views of woman suffrage were seen as "whims of my own" (John Stuart Mill, *Autobiography* [1874; reprint, Oxford: Oxford University Press, 1971], p. 169).

7. Samuel P. Huntington, *The Clash of Civilizations and the Remaking of the World Order* (New York: Simon & Schuster, 1996).

8. Quoted in the *International Herald Tribune*, August 27, 2004, p. 6.

9. This issue is discussed in chapters 4 and 8.

CHAPTER 2.

MAKING SENSE OF IDENTITY

1. V. S. Naipaul, *A Turn in the South* (London: Penguin, 1989), p. 33.
2. See also Leon Wieseltier, *Against Identity* (New York: Drenttel, 1996).
3. See my *On Ethics and Economics* (Oxford: Blackwell, 1987).
4. I have tried to discuss the intellectual limitations of this peculiarly imagined figure in parts of mainstream economics in "Rational Fools: A Critique of the Behavioral Foundations of Economic Theory," *Philosophy and Public Affairs* 6 (1977), reprinted in *Choice, Welfare and Measurement* (Oxford: Blackwell, 1982; Cambridge, Mass.: Harvard University Press, 1997), and also in Jane J. Mansbridge, ed., *Beyond Self-Interest* (Chicago: Chicago University Press, 1990).
5. See George Akerlof, *An Economic Theorist's Book of Tales* (Cambridge: Cambridge University Press, 1984); Shira Lewin, "Economics and Psychology: Lessons for Our Own Day from the Early 20th Century," *Journal of Economic Literature* 34 (1996); Christine Jolls, Cass Sunstein, and Richard Thaler, "A Behavioral Approach to Law and Economics," *Stanford Law Review* 50 (1998); Matthew Rabin, "A Perspective on Psychology and Economics," *European Economic Review* 46 (2002); Amartya Sen, *Rationality and Freedom* (Cambridge, Mass.: Harvard University Press, 2002), essays 1–5; Roland Benabou and Jean Tirole, "Intrinsic and Extrinsic Motivation," *Review of Economic Studies* 70 (2003).
6. See, among other contributions, George Akerlof and Rachel Kranton, "Economics and Identity," *Quarterly Journal of Economics* 63 (2000); John B. Davis, *The Theory of the Individual in Economics: Identity and Value* (London and New York: Routledge, 2003); Alan Kirman and Miriam Teschl, "On the Emergence of Economic Identity," *Revue de Philosophie Économique* 9 (2004); George Akerlof and Rachel Kranton, "Identity and the Economics of Organizations," *Journal of Economic Perspectives* 19 (2005).
7. See Jörgen Weibull, *Evolutionary Game Theory* (Cambridge, Mass.: MIT Press, 1995); Jean Tirole, "Rational Irrationality: Some Economics of Self-management," *European Economic Review* 46 (2002).
8. Karl Marx, *Critique of the Gotha Programme*, 1875; English translation in K. Marx and F. Engels (New York: International Publishers, 1938), p. 9.
9. Pierre Bourdieu, *Sociology in Question*, trans. Richard Nice (London: Sage, 1993), pp. 160–61.
10. E. M. Forster, *Two Cheers for Democracy* (London: E. Arnold, 1951).
11. On the relationship between the self and the community, see the illuminating analyses of Charles Taylor, *Sources of the Self and the Making of the Modern Identity* (Cambridge, Mass.: Harvard University Press, 1984), and *Philosophical Arguments* (Cambridge, Mass.: Harvard University Press, 1995). See also Will Kymlicka's insightful assessment of these and related issues in *Contemporary Political Philosophy: An Introduction* (Oxford: Clarendon Press, 1990).
12. For communitarian critiques of liberal theories of justice, see particularly Michael Sandel, *Liberalism and the Limits of Justice* (Cambridge: Cambridge University Press, 1982; 2nd ed., 1998); Michael Walzer, *Spheres of Justice* (New York: Basic Books, 1983); Charles Taylor, "Cross-Purposes: The Liberal-Communitarian Debate," in

Nancy L. Rosenblum, ed., *Liberalism and the Moral Life* (Cambridge, Mass.: Harvard University Press, 1989). See also John Rawls's response to criticisms of his theory of justice by Sandel and others in his "Justice as Fairness: Political Not Metaphysical," *Philosophy and Public Affairs* 14 (1985), and *Political Liberalism* (New York: Columbia University Press, 1993), to which Sandel responds in the 1998 edition of *Liberalism and the Limits of Justice*. Useful commentaries on these vigorous debates can be found in Will Kymlicka, *Contemporary Political Philosophy: An Introduction,* chapter 6; Michael Walzer, "The Communitarian Critique of Liberalism," *Political Theory* 18 (1990); Stephen Mulhall and Adam Swift, *Liberals and Communitarians* (Oxford: Blackwell, 1992, 1996). My skepticism of the communitarian critique of theories of justice is presented in *Reason Before Identity* (Oxford: Oxford University Press, 1999).

13. On this and related matters, see Frédérique Apffel Marglin and Stephen A. Marglin, eds., *Dominating Knowledge* (Oxford: Clarendon Press, 1993).

14. The role of dissent and argument in Indian traditions is discussed in my book *The Argumentative Indian* (London: Allen Lane; and New York: Farrar, Straus & Giroux, 2005).

15. Sandel, *Liberalism and the Limits of Justice,* pp. 150–51.

16. The ethics of identity is central to individual behavior precisely because of the inescapable choices about priorities over our many affiliations; on this, see Kwame Anthony Appiah's beautiful analysis in *The Ethics of Identity* (Princeton, N.J.: Princeton University Press, 2005). See also Amin Maalouf, *In the Name of Identity: Violence and the Need to Belong* (New York: Arcade Publishing, 2001)

CHAPTER 3.
CIVILIZATIONAL CONFINEMENT

1. Samuel P. Huntington, *The Clash of Civilizations and the Remaking of the World Order* (New York: Simon & Schuster, 1996).

2. Some of the issues discussed here are more fully investigated in my book *The Argumentative Indian* (London: Allen Lane; New York: Farrar, Straus & Giroux, 2005).

3. I discuss India's multireligious and multicultural history in *The Argumentative Indian*.

4. Huntington, *The Clash of Civilizations and the Remaking of the World Order,* p. 71.

5. Oswald Spengler, *The Decline of the West,* ed. Arthur Helps (New York: Oxford University Press, 1991), pp. 178–79.

6. See *Nihongi: Chronicles of Japan from the Earliest Times to* A.D. 697, trans. by W. G. Aston (Tokyo: Tuttle, 1972), pp. 128–33.

7. See Nakamura Hajime, "Basic Features of the Legal, Political, and Economic Thought of Japan," in Charles A. Moore, ed., *The Japanese Mind: Essentials of Japanese Philosophy and Culture* (Tokyo: Tuttle, 1973), p. 144.

8. Alexander responded, we learn from Flavius Arrian, to this egalitarian reproach with the same kind of admiration he had shown in his encounter with Diogenes, even though his own conduct remained altogether unchanged ("the exact opposite of what he then professed to admire"). See Peter Green, *Alexander of Macedon, 356–323 B.C.: A Historical Biography* (Berkeley: University of California Press, 1992), p. 428.

9. Alexis de Tocqueville, *Democracy in America,* trans. George Lawrence (Chicago: Encyclopaedia Britannica, 1990), p. 1.

10. Nelson Mandela, *Long Walk to Freedom* (Boston: Little, Brown, 1994), p. 21.

11. The significance of printing for public reasoning is discussed in my book *The Argumentative Indian,* pp. 82–83, 182–84.

CHAPTER 4.

RELIGIOUS AFFILIATIONS AND MUSLIM HISTORY

1. *Corpus of Early Arabic Sources for West African History,* trans. J. F. P. Hopkins, edited and annotated by N. Levtzion and J. F. P. Hopkins (Cambridge: Cambridge University Press, 1981), p. 285. See also *Ibn Battuta: Travels in Asia and Africa 1325–1354,* trans. H. A. R. Gibbs (London: Routledge, 1929), p. 321.

2. *Corpus of Early Arabic Sources for West African History,* p. 286; "Shariah" has been substituted here for Hopkins's abbreviated form "Shar'."

3. See Pushpa Prasad, "Akbar and the Jains," in Irfan Habib, ed., *Akbar and His India* (Delhi and New York: Oxford University Press, 1997), pp. 97–98.

4. The father of the Maratha king, Raja Sambhaji, whom the young Akbar had joined, was none other than Shivaji, whom the present-day Hindu political activists treat as a superhero, and after whom the intolerant Hindu party Shiv Sena is named (though Shivaji himself was quite tolerant, as the Mughal historian Khafi Khan, who was no admirer of Shivaji in other respects, reported).

5. See Iqtidar Alam Khan, "Akbar's Personality Traits and World Outlook: A Critical Reappraisal," in Habib, ed., *Akbar and His India,* p. 78.

6. María Rosa Menocal, *The Ornament of the World: How Muslims, Jews, and Christians Created a Culture of Tolerance in Medieval Spain* (New York: Little, Brown, 2002), p. 86.

7. Ibid., p. 85.

8. See Harry Eyres, "Civilization Is a Tree with Many Roots," *Financial Times,* July 23, 2005. As Jan Reed has noted, "Moorish irrigation works, later much extended, remain the basis for agriculture in the parched and dried regions of Spain and Portugal" (*The Moors in Spain and Portugal* [London: Faber & Faber, 1974], p. 235).

9. Reported by Michael Vatikiotis, "Islamizing Indonesia," *International Herald Tribune,* September 3–4, 2005, p. 5. See also Vatikiotis's "The Struggle for Islam," *Far Eastern Economic Review,* December 11, 2003, and M. Syafi'i Anwar, "Pluralism and Multi-culturalism in Southeast Asia: Formulating Educational Agendas and Programs," *ICIP Journal* 2 (January 2005).

10. There is also the related issue of how Islam should be interpreted in social and political contexts, including the need for a breadth of interpretation, on which see Ayesha

Jalal, *Self and Sovereignty: Individual and Community in South Asian Islam Since 1850* (London: Routledge, 2000). See also Gilles Kepel, *The War for Muslim Minds: Islam and the West* (Cambridge, Mass.: Harvard University Press, 2004).

11. The growing consolidation of a vigorous and largely independent media in Pakistan, dependent on the commitments of courageous and farsighted journalists, is a significant positive development for peace and justice in Pakistan that deserves much greater recognition than it tends to get outside the country. The tradition of reach and fearlessness established by such periodicals as the *Friday Times* (pioneered by the courageous and visionary Najam Sethi) and the *Herald,* and by dailies such as *The Dawn, The Nation,* the *Daily Times,* and the *News,* give reason for considerable hope for the future of the country. This would have pleased Faiz Ahmed Faiz, the great poet and distinguished early editor of the *Pakistan Times,* who worked hard for the development of an independent Pakistani media before it was blasted to bits by military rule and political extremism. He had to face incarceration, as did Najam Sethi later.

12. Husain Haqqani, "Terrorism Still Thrives in Pakistan," *International Herald Tribune,* July 20, 2005, p. 8. See also his insightful and informative book *Pakistan: Between Mosque and Military* (Washington, D.C.: Carnegie Endowment for International Peace, 2005). Also Ahmed Rashid, *Taliban: The Story of the Afghan Warlords* (London: Pan, 2001), and *Taliban: Islam, Oil and the New Great Game in Central Asia* (London: Tauris, 2002).

13. See the *Human Development Reports* published annually by the United Nations Development Programme, a project that was initiated, and for many years led, by Mahbub ul Haq. After Mahbub ul Haq's untimely death, this largely secular work has been carried out in Pakistan by an institute founded by him (which is now ably led by his widow, Khadija Haq).

14. Judea Pearl, "Islam Struggles to Stake Out Its Position," *International Herald Tribune,* July 20, 2005.

15. It is particularly relevant here to take note of the insightful distinction Mahmood Mamdani has presented with much clarity: "My aim is to question the widely held presumption . . . that extremist religious tendencies can be equated with political terrorism. Terrorism is not a necessary effect of religious tendencies, whether fundamentalist or secular. Rather, terrorism is born of political encounter" (*Good Muslim, Bad Muslim: America, the Cold War, and the Roots of Terror* [New York: Doubleday, 2004], pp. 61–62).

16. This is not to deny that the domain of Islamic tenets can be defined in somewhat different ways; see, for example, M. Syafi'i Anwar's distinction between the "legal-exclusive approach" and the "substantive-inclusive approach" in his paper "The Future of Islam, Democracy, and Authoritarianism in the Muslim World," *ICIP Journal* 2 (March 2005). But none of the variants can make religion a person's all-encompassing identity.

CHAPTER 5.
WEST AND ANTI-WEST

1. Albert Tevoedjre, *Winning the War Against Humiliation* (New York: UNDP, 2002), Report of the Independent Commission on Africa and the Challenges of the Third Millennium. This is the English translation of a report originally published in French: *Vaincre l'humiliation* (Paris, 2002).

2. William Dalrymple's engrossing novel about love across racial barriers in eighteenth-century India, *White Mughals* (London: Flamingo, 2002), when about a third of the British men in India were living with Indian women, would be hard to replicate in the century that followed, under increasingly hardened imperial relations.

3. James Mill, *The History of British India* (London, 1817; republished, Chicago: University of Chicago Press, 1975), p. 247.

4. Quoted in John Clive's introduction to Mill, *The History of British India,* p. viii.

5. Mill, *The History of British India,* pp. 225–26.

6. William Jones is often taken as a quintessential "Orientalist," which in an obvious sense he was. However, any proposal to find an overarching commonality of attitudes shared by all Orientalists—from William Jones to James Mill—would be hard to sustain. On this, see chapter 7 ("Indian Traditions and Western Imagination") of my book *The Argumentative Indian* (London: Allen Lane; New York: Farrar, Straus & Giroux, 2005).

7. Mill found in Jones's beliefs about early Indian mathematics and astronomy "evidence of the fond credulity with which the state of society among the Hindus was for a time regarded," and he was particularly amused that Jones had made these attributions "with an air of belief" (*The History of British India,* pp. 223–24). On the substantive side, Mill amalgamates the distinct claims regarding (1) the principle of gravitational attraction, (2) the daily rotation of the earth, and (3) the movement of the earth around the sun. Aryabhata's and Brahmagupta's concerns were mainly with the first two, on which specific assertions were made, unlike on the third.

8. Mill, *The History of British India,* pp. 223–24.

9. Ibid., p. 248.

10. *The Argumentative Indian,* chapters 6, 7, and 16.

11. Partha Chatterjee, *The Nation and Its Fragments* (Princeton, N.J.: Princeton University Press, 1993), p. 6.

12. On these and related issues, see also *The Argumentative Indian,* chapters 1–4 and 6–8.

13. Akeel Bilgrami, "What Is a Muslim?," in Anthony Appiah and Henry Louis Gates, eds., *Identities* (Chicago: University of Chicago Press, 1995).

14. Mamphela Ramphele, *Steering by the Stars: Being Young in South Africa* (Cape Town: Tafelberg, 2002), p. 15.

15. "Culture Is Destiny: A Conversation with Lee Kuan Yew," by Fareed Zakaria, *Foreign Affairs* 73 (March–April 1994), p. 113.

16. Quoted in the *International Herald Tribune,* June 13, 1995, p. 4. See also Lee's

insightful autobiography, *From Third World to First: The Singapore Story, 1965–2000*) (New York: HarperCollins, 2000).

17. W. S. Wong, "The Real World of Human Rights," speech made by the foreign minister of Singapore at the Second World Congress on Human Rights, Vienna, 1993.

18. Quoted in John F. Cooper, "Peking's Post-Tienanmen Foreign Policy: The Human Rights Factor," *Issues and Studies* 30 (October 1994), p. 69; see also Jack Donnelly, "Human Rights and Asian Values: A Defence of 'Western' Universalism," in Joanne Bauer and Daniel A. Bell, eds., *The East Asian Challenge for Human Rights* (Cambridge: Cambridge University Press, 1999).

19. I have discussed the evidence in *Human Rights and Asian Values: Sixteenth Morgenthau Memorial Lecture on Ethics and Foreign Policy* (New York: Carnegie Council on Ethics and International Affairs, 1997), republished in an abridged form in *The New Republic*, July 14 and 21, 1997. See also my book *Development as Freedom* (New York: Knopf; Oxford: Oxford University Press, 1999) and also "The Reach of Reason: East and West," *New York Review of Books*, July 20, 2000, reprinted in *The Argumentative Indian* (2005).

20. *Development as Freedom*, and also, jointly with Jean Drèze, *Hunger and Public Action* (Oxford: Clarendon Press, 1989).

21. Calculated from data presented by the Stockholm Peace Research Institute, http://www.sipri.org.

22. Kwame Anthony Appiah, *In My Father's House: Africa in the Philosophy of Culture* (London: Methuen, 1992), p. xii.

23. Meyer Fortes and Edward E. Evans-Pritchard, *African Political Systems* (New York: Oxford University Press, 1940), p. 12.

24. Appiah, *In My Father's House: Africa in the Philosophy of Culture*, p. xi.

25. Even when there are specific political movements with local concerns, such as the demands of Palestinians for their own territory and sovereignty, there are fundamentalist political readings of them which see those local confrontations as fitting into a general opposition to Western dominance, no matter how different such interpretations may be from the way most local people (in this case Palestinians) see the nature of what is involved in the specific regional dispute.

CHAPTER 6.
CULTURE AND CAPTIVITY

1. I have tried to have a go at that issue in "How Does Culture Matter?," in Vijayendra Rao and Michael Walton, eds., *Culture and Public Action* (Stanford, Calif.: Stanford University Press, 2004).

2. See Joel Mokyr's balanced assessment of this difficult issue in *Why Ireland Starved: A Quantitative and Analytical History of the Irish Economy, 1800–1850* (London: Allen

& Unwin, 1983), pp. 291–92. See also Mokyr's conclusion that "Ireland was considered by Britain as an alien and even hostile nation" (p. 291).

3. See Cecil Woodham-Smith, *The Great Hunger: Ireland, 1845–9* (London: Hamish Hamilton, 1962), p. 76.

4. See Andrew Roberts, *Eminent Churchillians* (London: Weidenfeld & Nicolson, 1994), p. 213.

5. Lawrence E. Harrison and Samuel P. Huntington, eds., *Culture Matters: How Values Shape Human Progress* (New York: Basic Books, 2000), p. xiii.

6. On this, see Noel E. McGinn, Donald R. Snodgrass, Yung Bong Kim, Shin-Bok Kim, and Quee-Young Kim, *Education and Development in Korea* (Cambridge, Mass.: Council on East Asian Studies, Harvard University, 1980).

7. William K. Cummings, *Education and Equality in Japan* (Princeton, N.J.: Princeton University Press, 1980), p. 17.

8. See Herbert Passin, *Society and Education in Japan* (New York: Teachers College Press, Columbia University, 1965), pp. 209–11; also Cummings, *Education and Equality in Japan*, p. 17.

9. Quoted in Shumpei Kumon and Henry Rosovsky, *The Political Economy of Japan*, vol. 3, *Cultural and Social Dynamics* (Stanford, Calif.: Stanford University Press, 1992), p. 330.

10. See Carol Gluck, *Japan's Modern Myths: Ideology in the Late Meiji Period* (Princeton, N.J.: Princeton University Press, 1985).

11. The inclusion of cultural freedom in the list of concerns of "human development" in the United Nations' *Human Development Report 2004* (New York: UNDP, 2004) is a substantial enrichment of the coverage of human development analysis.

12. See "Other People," published in the *Proceedings of the British Academy 2002*, and also as "Other People—Beyond Identity," *The New Republic*, December 18, 2000.

CHAPTER 7.

GLOBALIZATION AND VOICE

1. *The Advancement of Learning* (1605; reprinted in B. H. G. Wormald, *Francis Bacon: History, Politics and Science, 1561–1626* [Cambridge: Cambridge University Press, 1993]), pp. 356–57.

2. I discussed this issue in my commencement address ("Global Doubts") at Harvard University on June 8, 2000, published in *Harvard Magazine* 102 (August 2000).

3. T. B. Macaulay, "Indian Education: Minute of the 2nd February, 1835," reproduced in G. M. Young, ed., *Macaulay: Prose and Poetry* (Cambridge, Mass.: Harvard University Press, 1952), p. 722.

4. Howard Eves, *An Introduction to the History of Mathematics*, 6th ed. (New York: Saunders College Publishing House, 1990), p. 237. See also Ramesh Gangolli, "Asian Contributions to Mathematics," Portland Public Schools Geocultural Baseline Essay Series, 1999.

5. It must be acknowledged that Britain, under the leadership of Tony Blair and Gordon Brown, has played an important part in making the G8 countries move in that direction. Popular movements led by such colorful but sympathetic public figures as Bob Geldorf have also played an important part in generating support for such initiatives (despite the academic skepticism that often greets these resonant movements).

6. See Jeffrey Sachs, *The End of Poverty: How We Can Make It Happen in Our Lifetime* (London: Penguin Books, 2005).

7. My essay "Gender and Cooperative Conflict," in Irene Tinker, ed., *Persistent Inequalities* (New York: Oxford University Press, 1990), discusses the relevance and reach of the combination of cooperation and conflict.

8. See J. F. Nash, "The Bargaining Problem," *Econometrica* 18 (1950); Sylvia Nasar, *A Beautiful Mind* (New York: Simon & Schuster, 1999).

9. In fact, the pioneering theorists of the market economy, from Adam Smith, Leon Walras, and Francis Edgeworth to John Hicks, Oscar Lange, Paul Samuelson, and Kenneth Arrow, have tried to make clear that the market outcomes are deeply contingent on resource distribution and other determinants, and they—from Adam Smith onward—have proposed ways and means of making the arrangements more fair and just.

10. See Paul A. Samuelson, "The Pure Theory of Public Expenditure," *Review of Economics and Statistics* 35 (1954); Kenneth Arrow "Uncertainty and the Welfare Economics of Medical Care," *American Economic Review* 53 (1963); George Akerlof, *An Economic Theorist's Book of Tales* (Cambridge: Cambridge University Press, 1984); Joseph Stiglitz, "Information and Economic Analysis: A Perspective," *Economic Journal* 95 (1985).

11. On this, see George Soros, *Open Society: Reforming Global Capitalism* (New York: Public Affairs, 2000).

12. See, among other contributions, Joseph Stiglitz, *Globalization and Its Discontents* (London: Penguin, 2003), and Sachs, *The End of Poverty: How We Can Make It Happen in Our Lifetime*.

13. The ratio was 84.31 percent for the 1990s as a whole, according the findings of the Stockholm International Peace Research Institute, and the more recent figures indicate a consolidation, rather than any reversal, of this picture. The issue was discussed more fully in chapter 6. Of the G8 countries, only one (Japan) does not export any.

14. The Vaccine Board and the Global Alliance for Vaccines and Immunization have done much to make vaccines widely available in the poorer countries. A good example of an innovative proposal to increase the incentives for the development of such drugs is the possibility of offering preguaranteed bulk purchase through global NGOs and other international institutions that can be offered as a lure for medical research; see Michael Kremer and Rachel Glennerster, *Strong Medicine: Creating Incentives for Pharmaceutical Research on Neglected Diseases* (Princeton, N.J.: Princeton University Press, 2004).

15. The general problem of "global frontlines of modern medicine" is illuminatingly addressed by Richard Horton, *Health Wars* (New York: New York Review of Books,

2003). See also Paul Farmer, *Pathologies of Power: Health, Human Rights, and the New War on the Poor* (Berkeley: University of California Press, 2003), and Michael Marmot, *Social Determinants of Health: The Solid Facts* (Copenhagen: World Health Organization, 2003).

16. The role of public services in the equitable operation of market processes is discussed, with many illustrations, in my joint book with Jean Drèze, *India: Development and Participation* (Delhi and Oxford: Oxford University Press, 2002).

17. On this, see my "Sharing the World," *The Little Magazine* (Delhi) 5 (2004).

18. David Hume, *An Enquiry Concerning the Principles of Morals* (first published in 1777; republished, La Salle, Ill.: Open Court, 1966), p. 25.

CHAPTER 8.
MULTICULTURALISM AND FREEDOM

1. *Development as Freedom* (New York: Knopf; Oxford: Oxford University Press, 1999).

2. On shared U.S.-European problems, see also Timothy Garton Ash, *Free World: Why a Crisis of the West Reveals the Opportunity of Our Time* (London: Allen Lane, 2004).

3. James A. Goldston, "Multiculturalism Is Not the Culprit," *International Herald Tribune*, August 30, 2005, p. 6. For a different perspective, see also Gilles Kepel, *The War for Muslim Minds: Islam and the West* (Cambridge, Mass.: Harvard University Press, 2004), particularly chapter 7 ("Battle for Europe").

4. "Dumbed-Down GCSEs Are a 'Scam' to Improve League Tables, Claim Critics," by Julie Henry, *Daily Telegraph*, August 28, 2005, p. 1.

5. On the far-reaching relevance of hybridization in the contemporary world, see Homi Bhabha, *The Location of Culture* (New York: Routledge, 1994).

6. Agence France-Presse report, August 18, 2005.

7. The description here comes from the distinguished chair of the "Commission on the Future of Multi-ethnic Britain," Lord Parekh, in "A Britain We All Belong To," *Guardian*, October 11, 2000. There have been many other expressions of a similar kind, often demanding a "federal" system in a much cruder form. However, Bhikhu Parekh himself has insightfully presented other visions of multiculturalism in his own writings; see particularly *Re-thinking Multi-culturalism: Cultural Diversity and Political Theory* (Basingstoke: Palgrave, 2000).

8. See Cornelia Sorabji, *India Calling* (London: Nisbet, 1934), and Vera Brittain, *The Women at Oxford* (London: Harrap, 1960).

9. From the text of a press conference by Prime Minister Blair on July 26, 2005. Tony Blair shows a strong desire for cultural fairness in treating the newly established Islamic schools in the same way as the older Christian schools. That issue too was discussed in chapter 6.

10. See M. Athar Ali, "The Perception of India in Akbar and Abu'l Fazl," in Irfan Habib,

ed., *Akbar and His India* (Delhi: Oxford University Press, 1997), p. 220.

11. On the tradition of reasoning about alternative schools of religious thought (including agnosticism and atheism), see my book *The Argumentative Indian* (London: Allen Lane; New York: Farrar, Straus & Giroux, 2005).

12. From a press conference on July 26, 2005.

13. *Indian Round Table Conference (Second Session) 7th September, 1931–1st December, 1931: Proceedings* (London: Her Majesty's Stationery Office, 1932); see also C. Rajagopalachari and J. C. Kumarappa, eds., *The Nation's Voice* (Ahmedabad: Mohanlal Maganlal Bhatta, 1932).

14. M. K. Gandhi, "The Future of India," *International Affairs* 10 (November 1931), p. 739.

15. Aside from the barbarities involved in that terrible episode in Gujarat in 2002, the ideological issues brought out by that largely engineered violence (including the attempted rejection of Gandhiji's integrative ideas) are illuminatingly discussed by Rafiq Zakaria in *Communal Rage in Secular India* (Mumbai: Popular Prakashan, 2002).

16. *Indian Express*, August 13, 2005.

17. Thomas Friedman, *The World Is Flat* (New York: Farrar, Straus & Giroux, 2005). India's record in Kashmir in particular is, however, far less satisfactory. Kashmiri politics has suffered both from the invasion of terrorism from abroad and from rebellion at home.

CHAPTER 9.

FREEDOM TO THINK

1. See also his moving—and depressingly illuminating—book: Shaharyar M. Khan, *The Shallow Graves of Rwanda*, with a foreword by Mary Robinson (New York: I. B. Tauris, 2000).

2. See Will Kymlicka, *Contemporary Political Philosophy: An Introduction* (Oxford: Clarendon Press, 1990).

3. See "The Real News from Iraq," *Sunday Telegraph*, August 28, 2005, p. 24.

4. Derek Walcott, "Names," in *Collected Poems: 1948–1984* (New York: Farrar, Straus & Giroux, 1986).

NAMES INDEX

SUBJECT INDEX

PENGUIN PHILOSOPHY

THE ARGUMENTATIVE INDIAN
AMARTYA SEN

'Sen is unquestionably one of the most distinguished minds of our time ... The product of a great mind at the peak of its power, this is one of the most stimulating books about India to be written for years, and deserves the widest possible readership' William Dalrymple, *Sunday Times*

India is a country with many distinct pursuits, vastly different convictions, widely divergent customs and viewpoints. *The Argumentative Indian* brings together an illuminating selection of writings from Nobel prize-winning economist Amartya Sen that outline the need to understand contemporary India in the light of its long argumentative tradition.

Sen argues for the success of India's democracy, the defence of its secular politics, the removal of inequalities related to class, caste, gender and community, and the pursuit of sub-continental peace.

PENGUIN POLITICS

THE END OF POVERTY
JEFFREY SACHS

FOREWORD BY BONO

'The ideas in this book have a hook you won't forget: the end of poverty ... In Jeff's hands, the millstone of opportunity around our necks becomes an adventure, something doable and achievable' Bono

WE CAN END POVERTY BY 2025 ... AND CHANGE THE WORLD FOREVER.

For the first time in history, our generation has the opportunity to end extreme poverty in the world's most desperate nations. But how can we stop the cycle of bad health, bad debt, and bad luck that holds back more than a billion people?

Jeffrey D. Sachs, Special Advisor to UN Secretary-General Kofi Annan and 'probably the most important economist in the world' (*The New York Times*) has the answers. He has visited and worked in over 100 countries across the globe – from Africa to India, Poland to Bolivia – advising leaders on economic development and poverty reduction. Here he lays out how poverty has been beaten in the past, how – in realistic, attainable steps – we can make a real difference for the one-fifth of humanity who still live in extreme poverty, how they can find partnership with their wealthy counterparts, how little it will actually cost, and how everyone can help.

The End of Poverty is a roadmap to a more prosperous and secure world.